YOU

Come First

How To Finally Live The Life You Know You Deserve

By

Dr. Noel Gordon

Wherever your heart finds brightness in times of solitude is an indication of where it truly belongs.

For more information, contact Dr. Noel Gordon at email drnoelgordon1@gmail.com or website www.drnoelgordon.com.

ISBN: 978-1-7359156-0-9

Published in the United States

By

Dr. Noel Gordon

NoelGordon Publishing

Dedication

This book is dedicated to my parents,
Charles Agustus Gordon (Pops) and Eileen McPherson-Gordon
(Miss Darling), whose spirits continue to sustain me.

Acknowledgements

---- ★ ✦ ★ ----

This book became a reality because of the consistent indulgence of the following individuals:

Jodine Gordon, my daughter who offered her uncensored critical review and made numerous valuable recommendations which were taken into account as I completed the final version of the manuscript.

Hyacinth Gordon-Clarke, my sister who proofread several chapters of the manuscript, and served as my primary cheerleader, especially whenever I lacked motivation.

Dennard Mitchell, my writing coach whose guidance and inspiration served as a catalyst that made the vision of writing this book a reality.

Winston Lawrence, who dedicated quality time to proofread the manuscript on several occasions to ensure accuracy of the content.

As you approach the next season of your life, step into this new era with a renewed resolve and commitment. Your first priority should be YOU. Focus on adequately maintaining the four essential dimensions of life that allow for optimal living. These are the PHYSICAL, MENTAL, SPIRITUAL, and SOCIAL dimensions. Deliberately take the necessary steps to maintain a healthy physical and mental existence. Relentlessly pursue and embrace an authentic and objective spiritual reality. Enhance your social awareness, and venture out into new and exciting social arenas. The evolution of the four dimensions of life is intrinsically motivated and, therefore, not governed by external compulsions. Do not be bothered, deterred, or intimated by your past, present, or future. Be grateful for my past and be hopeful for a great future. LIVE in the present. Enthusiastically embrace all aspects of your life!

Table of Contents

———— ★ ★ ★ ————

Forward

— ★ ★ ★ —

T he title of this book is an irrefutable indicator of the system of values which have been cherished and upheld by its author - Dr. Noel Gordon. This set of values did not emerge during the phase of his adult life. Instead, they were planted in his childhood, nurtured and pruned in his adolescence, and now made to flourish at this stage of his life when physical growth is receding and the proclivity towards youthful adventures has given way to prudent behavior and a matured outlook. His own life experiences, coupled with his professional and academic attainments, render him eligible to inspire hope and courage in others. This he does without need for caution or thought of reckless repercussions.

Dr. Gordon's goal is that of drawing from his deep well of experiences to inspire and uplift those of his readers who are no strangers to life's vicissitudes and calamities. His instruments of faith, along with his solid moral precepts, are deeply embedded throughout the pages of this book. The reader is faced with an option. Read the entire book in sequence of chapters, or turn to the table of contents and select a page or section, as remedy to the pressures which life brings. Whichever option one chooses, the answer will be derived from a source that is credible, believable, and authentic.

It is a widely held view, that the average individual gravitates towards books that are authored with the interest of the reader in mind. This book captures that mantra in full. Within it, is a plethora of views and statements that can undergird the efforts of professionals – such as: counselors, therapists, or the clergy – just to name a few. Yet, its content is current and relevant to make it suited for other readers whose only desire is that of picking up a good book to nurture the soul, and provide inspiration for a moment when life seems unbearable and the hope of a brighter tomorrow appears as a mirage.

I therefore believe that the general readership of this book will fall within two broad categories. First, there will be those readers who will likely select this text as a reliable source of inspirational reading within an informal and leisurely setting. Secondly, one can readily see this text being utilized by groups of individuals in study sessions, as a means of engaging thought without having the desire to indoctrinate or influence anyone. Its content is broad-based and objective, thereby holding the potential of serving a unitary purpose without need for follow-up persuasion or indoctrination.

Of recent, there is an apparent trend among matured individuals to extrapolate from certain texts, common themes or ideas in an effort aimed at building social networks and promoting academic inquiry. This trend has been heightened over the period of time in which society has been enveloped by the effects of the COVID–19 pandemic. The restrictions which have appeared as an aftermath of that phenomenon, has left many persons lonely, sad, and despondent. Luckily, social media, and the variety of technological platforms which have emerged to accommodate synchronous learning, are now playing a significant role in that regard, while keeping individuals in touch with one another. Such developments have helped to sustain the appetite of persons who want to participate in "book talks." However, for these networking opportunities to remain sustainable there has to be a set of resources to which they can refer to obtain meaningful and substantive views and ideas. To those individuals, I absolutely recommend this book. I do so with the knowledge that, in spite of the variance in approach by its readers, persons who select this book for discussion purposes, will find it to entail a repertoire of information which can be easily harnessed and brought to bear to a lively and thought-provoking conversation at the bat of a hat.

When I first acquainted myself with this book, chapter one gripped my attention with the same commanding tone of my childhood headmaster who saw within me the potential that could lift me up beyond the ordinary and propel me to a higher range of achievement in life. Interestingly, that was not all. As I read further, each chapter appeared to me as though it were my personal counselor, telling me how best to navigate the maze which comes along with being alive in a modern world that is ever changing its norms with the expectations that I too will follow. By the time I arrived at the last chapter, I had undergone a series of pondering and reflections which forced me to look squarely at life in a new way and with the prospect of experiencing a brighter tomorrow.

Glad am I to have read this book, which leads me to my final point. Purchase it and read it also. Keep it close to you at the place where you normally go to find solace, peace, and tranquility when the storms of life are raging. It is a handy guide for a quick reading at bed-time, or a reference guide when one travels away from home. Once one has read this book, one can no longer believe that there is no hope of a brighter tomorrow. Instead, one will likely ask one's self, as I did: "Where was this book when I was faced with that issue which was so burdensome and so personal for me to share with anyone?"

Collin M. Wolfe, Ed.D.
Dr. Colin M. Wolfe is a Principal
New York City Public School

Author's Note

★ ★ ★

Tuesday, February 14, 2017 was a momentous day in my life. That was the day when my 20 years as a career public school educator, 12 of which were spent as a district administrator, came under scrutiny. That was the last day I spent on my job, until three years later when I was exonerated of the false allegations, and officially reinstated as a district administrator, on Thursday, February 13, 2020. I give credit to this experience for providing me with the inspiration to write this book.

The word 'relevance' should not only be a part of our vocabulary but its essence should be intentionally considered and incorporated into every facet of our lives. Are we fully vested in all the engagements that occupy our daily lives? Do we fully understand and embrace our motives for these engagements? Are we embracing the status quo at the expense of our individuality, desires, values, and happiness? As you ponder your response to these questions, you should become acutely aware that, as the steward of your life, you owe it to yourself to chart your own course. In their quest to navigate life's complex and meandering realities, people oftentimes, purposefully or unwittingly, become dependent on and guided by the perspectives, convictions, and dictates of others. Please be aware that everyone comes to the table with personal agendas, and those agendas are usually self-centered and self-serving; hence, be careful to remain resolute in your quest to fulfill your destiny.

You should live in the realm of your authentic self. You should refrain from allowing yourself to be governed by the expectations or judgments of your environment. One of the most significant and empowering hallmarks a person striving for wholesomeness can attain in this life, is to arrive at the point where other people's subjective perceptions and personal convictions do not color or dictate one's self concept, deter one's aspirations, infringe on one's peace of mind, or impose on one's identity and dignity. Do not be concerned about fitting in. Embrace your own ideals and stand confidently.

As you work towards a better representation of yourself, you should strive to live in the realm of your true identity, and consistently demonstrate all that you currently embody. In the interim, do not suspend the celebration of yourself for a future that is unguaranteed. While you appreciate and celebrate life, you should be intentional in your quest for objectivity, your advocacy for tolerance, your respect for individuality, your abhorrence of mediocrity, and your mission for self-actualization. As you journey towards your destiny, seek to be empowered with the will and competencies to lead a balanced, meaningful, harmonious, and fulfilled life.

Noel Gordon, Ed.D.

Chapter 1

Keep It Real

It's Your Life So Direct Your Own Story

— ★ ★ ★ —

Don't live based on the desires and dictates of others and develop a practical and attainable strategic plan for your own life. Do not limit your aspirations based on the apprehensions of others or the prevailing nuances of your circumstances. With determination, you can accomplish phenomenal feats far beyond the scope of your current reality.

Authenticity

I was invited to participate in a college information session that was hosted at the Meadowlands in New Jersey. The participants were asked to submit a copy of their business cards, and later on, cards were randomly selected. My card was selected, and I received an authenticated Vince Carter Number 15 Jersey. I was assured of the authentication because the jersey was accompanied by an authentication letter signed by Vince Carter, the famous basketball player. My host handed me the letter which validated the authenticity of the jersey. I was told that in years to come, the jersey would be of even greater value.

Let us examine authentication. Whether we are self-employed, employed by a corporation or whatever our vocation, we are faced with the unwritten rule to align ourselves with convention. We are pressured to play a role in order to be accepted. I find that, in many instances, people do not function as authentically as they would like to be. Sometimes, because of the prevailing culture of our environment, we act according to the expectations of those around us. For political reasons, or for whatever other motivations, individuals may experience some level of pressure on their secular jobs, so they are challenged to compromise their authenticity. People may want acceptance, and so they compromise their values. It is often very difficult to find people who really display the level of authenticity that truly represents their true values. For those who strive to be themselves, and for those who neglect the undesirable dictates of their environment, there is a lot of pressure. Those who seek to abide by the values that they have established for themselves are sometimes the ones who are perceived as adversarial or going against the grain. Going against the grain may be an unwitting response. They may not be intentional in going against the grain, but when they purpose to be themselves, then the compromising personalities within the system become offended, oppositional, or judgmental.

I want to first start with the religious environment because I embraced that culture during my most impressionable years. I was age 16 when I was exposed, in an intimate way, to a fundamentalist legalistic religious system. For most of my life, I lived in a manner that every decision I made, every step that I took, and every response that I gave to a question or situation, was contingent upon how I would be construed by those in this particular religious system. There were subjective rules, dogmas and cultural norms espoused by the adherents of this religious system. As a member of this system, you may not even be remotely in agreement with some of these rules and dogmas, but you are compelled to embrace every aspect of the system in order to ensure acceptance. Even though there might not necessarily be an explicit biblical reference or a sound theological construct that supported a particular religious perspective, adherents of this system blindly adhered to the tenets of the construct. They did so because they desired to maintain the status quo within the community.

If you are not mindful of the dangers inherent in thoughtless submission, then as time goes by, you lose your objectivity and sense of self. I am sure that this resonates with some individuals, particularly those who may be apprehensive in publicly articulating their objective perspective surrounding this matter. During my tenure in that setting, I lost my identity and embraced ideals that I knew in my heart were neither logical, theologically sound, nor reasonable. These ideals had nothing to do with biblical instructions or authentic spirituality. I lost myself by adhering to principles which were inconsistent with my core values. If you are living in a space where you are controlled by a system that is steeped in subjectivity, a system that manipulates you mentally, and a system that controls your life, then you are not living authentically. It took me about 30 years to really understand that I was not living my life authentically. I was not living my best life. I was not living in a space where I could independently own my decisions and give my uncensored responses, based on my personal convictions.

Independent Thinking

Systems reinforce themselves via feedback loops that reward behaviors that perpetuate the ideals of the system and "punish" behaviors that are antithetical to the system. The system that was controlling my mind did not really and truly encourage or demonstrate the critical thinking skills that foster independent thinking. It intended to maintain the status quo and any potential threat to the status quo was misconstrued as rebellion. The adherents to such a system were required to embrace norms that would meet the demands of the system's ideals and practices that would ensure the survival and perpetuation of the system in its existing state. Many people are so caught up with rituals and subjective propaganda inherent in organized religion. They are so caught up with the tenets of religion that they have not only lost their sense of self but also lost the ability or willingness to think critically, rationally, or objectively.

If the religious practitioner does not embrace a doctrinal position in its entirety or if the dress code is inconsistent with the one established by the religious culture, then shunning is imminent. Consequently, people feel pressured into acting and dressing in a particular way. Modesty and sacredness are essentially based on the perception of the masses within the community. I happened to travel to Zimbabwe, Southern Africa, and I remember traveling for many hours through the deep rural areas. I remember seeing people who were very sparingly attired. Their attire, even though it brought no offence to their fellow countrymen, would be regarded as grossly immodest in mainstream western culture. The values espoused by a balanced faith community should be universal and replicable in all geographical locations. These values should not be based on the outward appearance but on the regenerated condition of the heart. It would be reductive to think I am advocating for immodesty. I am speaking to the fact that if the focus is on externalities, then the possibility of genuine spirituality could be woefully compromised.

Pseudo-self

Living your life is like writing a story in your heart and displaying it on the stage of life. You should ensure that your action on stage is consistent with the written story in your heart. It is human nature to project positive things and give others the impression that you are fine and that everything is balanced and going in the right direction. From many years of working in various aspects of human relations, I have discovered that people tend to display their persona. People put forward the parts of themselves that they would like for others to see and the parts they think would be appreciated and admired. They give the impression that all is well in all aspects of their lives. Particularly in the social media culture, the things that people project are designed to give a very positive impression. It should be your desire to really live a life in which you can be true to yourself. Embrace the creed by William Shakespeare that says, *'To thine own self be true.'* You can become a slave to the desire of living your life to please others, and if you are not careful, you could live your life solely to impress others. This is generally done to seek approval and acceptance of the masses. Others may be pleased with the way you navigate through the public arena, but this display could be done at the expense of your realness and to your eventual demise.

When you are locked away and evaluate yourself, what is reflected back to you should be consistent with the story that is written on your heart. Commit to spending the rest of your life in a place where you are able to look in the mirror and see the reflection of the best version of yourself. At the end of the day, you have the choice to live your life in a manner that your actions are a true reflection of your values and world view. If you continue to live your life just to please others or just to be accepted by others, eventually, you will no longer be able to identify your true self. When you cannot recognize the person in the mirror, then your credibility could be at stake. There is no crime in being your true self. There is no crime in you living a life that reflects your personal values. There is also no crime in making choices that are good for you even though they may not necessarily be approved by others.

Mind Your Business

Be mindful that the public largely assesses and judges based on its own expectations. You should make your own choices. If the public chooses to fall in line with the choices that you make for your life, then that is a desirable bonus; however, it should not be the determining factor in making your decisions. If your greatest need is to be accepted by others, then you will eventually sacrifice too much of your original self to accommodate that need. Your greatest need should be to fulfill your potential, and working towards accomplishing the steps that lead towards the fulfillment of your destiny. Every human is given a specific path that leads to a unique destination. You have been given the necessary resources to accomplish your goals in life. Some people have not used their resources efficiently. Some people become dependent on others to show them the way. Some individuals have curtailed their personal journey to assist others in accomplishing their personal goals. Many have spent the time allotted to them on earth in making sure others' dreams are fulfilled, to the detriment of their own dreams. They will ultimately realize that they are performing on someone else's stage, in a lead role, as an actor in that person's story. This will undoubtedly leave them unfulfilled, unaccomplished, disoriented, and dejected. Hopefully, if not too late, they will come to terms with their loss of focus and get back on their own stage.

Everybody comes to the table with a personal agenda. No one is excluded. The agenda can be positive, negative, selfless, or self-centered. Human beings are intrinsically built for self-preservation and survival; hence, it is not common for people to consciously prioritize the needs of others over theirs. In my experience, those who display such empathetic attributes are susceptible to manipulation and abandonment. There is a biblical principle that says we should love our neighbors as we love ourselves. We are not required to love anyone more intensely than we love ourselves. Some people's desire to please others is so intense that they are inclined to do so at the expense of their own essential needs. Neglecting of one's essential needs is not a positive trait. You should place yourself at the top of your priority list. Focus on the things that will substantially cater to your personal affairs. You should focus on the things that will allow you to actualize your potential and keep you on track towards your destiny.

I have had conversations with a number of individuals who have gone through their 30s, some who have gone through their 40s, and others who have gone through their 50s. They arrived at a point in their lives where they discovered that they were not embracing their true selves. They were left unfulfilled, empty, lost and in a dark place. One of these persons indicated to me that he had ultimately lost his identity. When you ignore yourself and focus on others, you will eventually be forced to question your priorities. Are you at a point where you have done everything for everybody and nothing life-transforming for yourself? You might have dedicated your entire life to raising your children or you might have literally lived a life that caters exclusively to the needs of your children. You did all you could for them, but they are gone, and now you have an empty nest. You might have worked as a committed member of staff for an employer for many years, and you got to a stage where you were looking forward to retirement, but staff reduction or reorganization resulted in you losing your job and your hope for a substantial retirement package. Your employers eliminated your job, and you are left with an altered existence and a crippling emptiness. You might not have lost your job but decided to retire and left unfulfilled. I have spoken with a number of retirees who grappled to find themselves and make meaning of their post-retirement lives. I participated in a retirement conference some time ago, and the facilitator warned the participants that they should be very strategic in developing a retirement plan. He said that retirement was not a pleasant experience for everybody. He said that it was not practical for the retiree to have expectations of involvement in an unlimited number of entertaining activities. They should acquire new skills and hobbies and engage in other consequential and fulfilling activities.

Self-interest

Nothing on earth should take precedence over your self-care because, at some point in time, you are going to be relieved of the many responsibilities that you prioritize over yourself. Your children are on a short-term loan to you. They eventually leave the nest to establish their own lives. Your job is temporary, even if you are a business owner. As much as you may want to think so, you are not the priority of your relatives, friends, and associates. I have encountered several unfortunate occurrences in my life, and I realized that, for the most part, I was on my own in my effort to be on track with my life and livelihood. Some empathic individuals may put forth their best effort and lend support to varying degrees. Others who you thought would be there to lend their support will be missing in action. You are your own most loyal supporter, and you should do whatever it takes to ensure that your most loyal supporter makes you the number one priority.

These days, people are living to a good old age. A growing number of people live to their 70s, 80s, and even 90s. Many amazing people spent their working years laboring for people around them and living for their children and they never made adequate provision to meet their needs during their senior years. Take stock of your life today and make sure that your plans and actions are geared towards making you the main interest. They should be structured to ensure your security and fulfillment. You should seek to engage in activities that enhance your inner peace. Enjoy the moments of your day and every step that you take along your journey. Ensure that you are truly happy and that you are at peace with yourself. Make sure that your smiles and laughter are a true reflection of your internal reality. Never sacrifice your own peace of mind and security to facilitate the peace of mind and security of others. There is a thin line between sacrifice and self-deprivation.

Do not allow others to withdraw from your resources without ensuring the rejuvenation of your own resources. If people keep drawing from you and there are no provisions for replenishment, you will become depleted and left in a state of emptiness. Many individuals today are on overdraft and having to function in the negative domain. I am not just talking about financial or other material resources, I am also talking about emotional resources. When everything is taken from you without being replenished, then you will become diminished, and the representation of your true self is distorted. Sadly, it takes such a dilemma for some individuals to wake up to the impairment and unfortunate outcome of self-mismanagement. It is only at this rock-bottom stage that some individuals truly see the urgency for rejuvenation and refocus on self.

My school district once adopted a practice that was called the *Drop Everything and Read* activity. All the teachers and students in the various schools throughout the district were required to stop whatever they were doing and read. A drop-everything and focus-on-self practice might be the best thing for you to adopt immediately. There comes a time when it is best for you to stop what you are doing and realign your course of action with your personal welfare as your priority. Stop what you are doing and examine whether your actions are aligned with your desires and values. It could be that you are acting from a place of unhappiness, joylessness, boredom, self-destructive routines, or lack of fulfillment. Such a mode of operation leads to misery. If your ability to function has deteriorated to the point of incapacitation, then you need to start taking stock of yourself and make the necessary positive changes. You do not want to find yourself in such an unfortunate position. When you get to this depth of dismay, it is very difficult to elevate yourself. This place will require you to go to therapy, revisit your action plan, and make changes that are geared towards self-fulfillment.

When you are dealing with adversity, it can be easy to assume that you are invincible and that you will automatically overcome the problem; consequently, you are left alone to struggle. This assumption could be as a result of you projecting yourself as the savior for everyone around you. You may not intentionally project yourself in that manner, but people draw their conclusion based on their perception of your behavior. Some will think that you are always fine when you are not. It took me a long while to embrace my own vulnerabilities, but I have learned to do so. I am learning more and more to say that I am not okay whenever I am not okay. I have also learned to say that things are not fine with me when they are actually not fine. My approach to life, and for what I am planning on doing in the future, is that I will be operating from a position of vulnerability and authenticity. When I approach people from a position of vulnerability, then I am more relatable, and my genuine self provides the illumination that they need to find their way.

Points to Ponder

a. Be comfortable with yourself

    i.   Acknowledge your limitations

    ii.   Seek professional help in developing areas in need of improvement

    iii.   Celebrate and build on your strengths

b. Validate yourself

    i.   Engage in self-examination of your competencies and values

    ii.   Recognize your areas of strength and challenges

    iii.   Acknowledge your strengths and challenges

c. Be a non-conformist

    i.   Ask clarifying question and demand answers

    ii.   Determine the rationality of responses based on your outlook

    iii.   Respond based on your conviction and not on public opinion

d. Be unafraid of failure

    i.   Be comfortable with the fact that we are susceptible to failure

   ii.   Come to terms with the fact that you will fail at something

   iii.   See your failures as teachable moments

e. Be an independent thinker

   i.   Never be unconditionally compliant

   ii.   Endorse agendas that align with your conviction

   iii.   Disassociate from agendas that are incompatible with your conviction

Embrace and celebrate life. Be PRESENT and fully engaged in every notable occurrence because it's the MOMENTS that really count. Learn from the past, be inspired by the present, and be positively expectant of the future. Do not allow the past or the future to infringe on the prospects of the present.

Reflections

_____

_____

_____

_____

_____

_____

_____

_____

_____

_____

_____

_____

_____

_____

_____

_____

_____

_____

_____

Chapter 2

Respect Yourself
Activate And Utilize Your Power Of Self-respect

───────── ★ ★ ★ ─────────

Self-respect is generated and nurtured from within. It is based on the beliefs that you accept about yourself and your reaction to the judgments of others. It is not the things around you, such as the material acquisition, approvals and the affirmations, which determine the level of respect you have for yourself. It is an intrinsic qualifier.

Self-pride

Respect is having great admiration for someone or something. Self-respect is having pride or confidence in you. It gives you the feeling that you are behaving with honor and dignity. Some people believe that self-respect is synonymous with pride. Some people think that pride is a bad quality to possess, but it also has a positive connotation. Pride, whether positive or negative, has its implications. Self-pride is a good value. Some teachings suggest that you should not think highly of yourself, but I contend that you should think highly of yourself. If you do not, then who will? You should think of yourself as special, and you should embrace the perspective that no one in this world is better than you are. No one in this world should be more special to you than yourself.

There are different individuals with different abilities and opportunities. These merits may manifest themselves in a manner that shows certain individuals in a positive light, as compared to others. This does not give individuals a license to think of themselves as better off, or worse off, than others. Your innate or acquired endowments do not give you permission to look down on a less fortunate human being. You need to take pride in your natural or nurtured attributes and opportunities and affirm yourself regularly. Look in the mirror and tell yourself that you are an amazing human being. Cultivate and manifest your self-pride and be assertive about it. You ought to be proud of yourself. Represent yourself well.

You should not adjust your authentic self to fit into anyone's agenda. To the contrary, others should be willing to respect and accommodate your standards. Maintain your standards even under duress. That is a very important rule of thumb. It is critical that you understand and embrace the power of self-pride. In order to excel and execute efficiently in life, it is vital that you admire, embrace and love yourself. If you admire yourself, then rational people will appreciate you without an inclination to force you into changing who you are.

Self-image

Have you ever been in a room where someone's arrival brought a lightness and brightness to the space, without them having to say anything? Such an experience often leaves you with precious memories. Have you ever been in the presence of an individual and felt repulsed? Have you ever been in the presence of an individual and pick up on some negative vibes? You emit energy in your immediate surroundings and also in the atmosphere. Your energy can be an indicator of your self-image. The type of energy that you radiate will be reflected back to you. If you send out negative energy, then negative energy will come back to you. If you send out positive energy, then positive energy will likely be returned to you. Your energy is not only emitted through spoken words. You do not even have to open your mouth to unleash your energy. Your very presence discharges your energy. Your facial expression, your body language, and your non-verbal communication are reflectors of your energy and self-image.

If you find yourself in a negative environment, you should feel no obligation to remain in such toxic space. You should regard yourself enough to move away from negativity. You do not have to be the one constantly making adjustments to tolerate undesirable energies and noxious personalities. Every person who is born on the face of the earth has a right to be here. Once you are here, you have the same human rights as everybody else. I do understand that civilization and socio-economic realities tend to influence our outlook. If you are not careful, the circumstances of life could cause you to arrive at irrational conclusions concerning your self-image. Do not look outside of yourself for the ideal image. You have an obligation to develop and own positive thoughts and reviews about yourself or any other matter. Celebrate your virtues. You do not have to attempt to be like other persons.

Many years ago, after graduating from junior college, I was gainfully employed with an organization which required us to be in the field on a regular basis. I developed a good professional relationship with my coworkers, even though I was not as matured. They were either grown men, most already graduated from university, or were older men, some with children and grandchildren. One day we were asked to give our opinion on a matter, and all my coworkers enthusiastically gave their personal opinions. When it became my turn to give my opinion, I indicated that I would be in support of the ultimate outcome, whatever it turned out to be. I remember quite candidly how upsetting my response was to one of my colleagues. He told me emphatically that I should not just go along with the flow but have an opinion of my own. At the time of my reprimand I felt disparaged, but later on I reflected on the matter and realized that he was correct in confronting me in this regard. I was actually uncomfortable to present an opinion that could be offensive to any of my coworkers. During that stage of my life, I wanted to be in the good graces of everyone and so I was hesitant to take a position that may offend others. Following that experience, I learned to value and state my opinion when appropriate, and not be intimidated by the possibility of counteraction. A challenging or disappointing phase of your journey should not diminish the vision of what you aspire to accomplish in life. Follow the meandering path of your ordained destiny and be empowered by your encounters. Follow your own path and learn from every aspect of your unique journey.

Self-respect does not come from external endorsements; it is generated and nurtured from within. It is based on the beliefs that you accept about yourself and your reaction to the judgments of others. It is not the things around you which should determine the level of respect you have for yourself. The problem is that people sometimes wait for those in their various social circles to validate them. If you sit back and wait for someone to admire and validate you, it may never happen. It is unadvisable to sit back, waiting for someone to shower you with accolades. No one should be given the power to decide how you feel about yourself. Your perception of yourself should come from a healthy mindset.

Look within the deep recesses of your heart. Look within the enclaves of your spirit. Look within your core beliefs. Look at how you value yourself. How do you see yourself? Do you see yourself as a phenomenal person or do you form an impression of yourself based on the subjective dictates of others or society? Do you subject yourself to the judgments of toxic individuals armed with self-serving motives? Do you tend to succumb to the wishes of those who have the tendency to impose on your physical and mental spaces blatantly and consistently? Whose influence have you allowed to frame the impression you have of yourself? Who invaded your life and devalued your dignity?

There are influential individuals in society who can pollute the positive perception you have of yourself. Your advancement is based on how much you allow these entities to manipulate your mind and devalue your worth. Certain people will be generous in accentuating their perceived negative judgments about you and withhold their applause for the positives that you represent. If you are an admirable person and you have accomplished major feats, yet no one ever affirms you, then you could potentially be led to doubt your own capabilities and devalue your self-confidence. Dysfunctional people will attempt to transfer their incapability and insufficiencies to you. Listen carefully. They are telling you how they really feel about themselves. To understand who people are, just listen to the things that they articulate. Hold the people who matter to you accountable when they erroneously indict you. Hold people accountable for attempting to describe your contribution to a cause as inconsequential when the evidence has proven otherwise. If people attempt to undervalue your worth, be unperturbed and maintain your confidence. Some individuals want you to think of yourself in the same negative manner that they think of themselves. Do not buy into this imposition. Have confidence in the positive self-image that you have cultivated for yourself.

Self-protection

Ignore individuals who make it their mission to say negative things about you. Do not take it personally. They may infer or tell you that you can do nothing right. They may even give the inaccurate impression that you are a negative person. For such toxic individuals, it does not matter how well-intended your motive is, they will twist it in a manner for it to appear ulterior. They will make inaccurate assumptions about you based on their false impressions, and then try to convince you and others that these indictments are accurate. These are narcissistic tendencies. Many good people have unintentionally invited narcissistic people into their lives. Beware of such individuals because they grapple with layers of dysfunctionalities. They will invade your space and create a crescendo of hurt and pain that you could never imagine. You did not intentionally invite such chaos into your life, and by the time you realize what you are being subjected to, it is too late to make a swift retreat. This kind of invasion can potentially pose a major threat to your sanity, your resources, and your self-respect. If this harmful scenario becomes a reality in your life, then you should promptly plan an exit strategy and rapidly get away from such an unfavorable entanglement. Make it the norm to always err on the side of caution in an effort to preserve your dignity. Be warned! It is better to be safe than sorry. If necessary, make the decision to leave the situation with your intellect, follow through with your plans, and wait on your heart and emotions to eventually follow. Run for your life if you are ever entangled with a narcissist personality. Protection of your sanity and self-respect should be among your most important and non-negotiable priorities.

Have you ever been caught in a circumstance that transformed you, from a mentally healthy person full of joy and aspirations, into an emotionally traumatized person that you can hardly recognize? Have you been confronted by someone who insists on convincing you to embrace what they assume you are thinking or feeling, when you know for sure that you were neither thinking nor feeling what they assumed? They are actually attempting to project their thoughts and feelings on you. There could be several things going on here. They could be projecting their feelings onto you without any basis. Their intention might be genuinely positive, but the impact of their actions could be harmful, even though they did not intend for it to be. If they care about people, they should not shirk away from taking responsibility for their harmful actions, even if they did not intend to cause harm. Credible persons will be accountable by evaluating the merits of their behavior and make amends when needed. No personal or business relationship is worth the erosion of your wholesomeness. No association is worth the corrosion of your peace. No family dynamic is worth the destruction of your joyfulness. No personal desire is worth the sacrifice of your serenity. There is infinite power in self-preservation. Avoid the clutter and give yourself time and space to focus on maintaining your emotional health.

I once had a friend who would constantly tell me about the negative things a colleague would say about me. At first, I was curious, but eventually, I began to feel uncomfortable. I asked the friend why this colleague had such a level of comfort engaging him in such discourses. You should always watch the messenger. I told the friend to stop informing me about these matters, but the request was not heeded. This triangulation came to an end when I asked a mutual friend to speak with the person who allegedly said the negative things about me. The message I sent was that I heard about these negative assertions from his friend and, if that were the case, I was asking that he desist from doing so. I effectively terminated a negative scenario that could potentially upset my peace of mind. Protect your peace, even if it costs you friendships and associations. I understand that people have their own issues, and hurting people will hurt people, but we should always choose not to be a casualty of anyone's dysfunction.

Do not employ someone else as your standard-bearer. If so, you may fall below the level of their standard. Set your own standards. Be assured of what you represent and embrace it with conviction. You may inadvertently hurt others. In such cases, face the reality of your misstep and course correct without making it a judgment on who you are. Emulate the good you see in others, but never compare yourself with others.

Your self-concept is influenced by several variables. It comes from the way you were raised, and particularly from the way you were influenced by your significant others during your most impressionable years. Aim to protect and enhance your self-concept. There may have been a time when you did not feel very good about yourself because of external or internal factors. If you allow negativity to marinate in your mind, it will unconstructively influence the way you see yourself. As I grew from childhood to adulthood, I came to the conclusion that everyone had limitations. In my early years in high school, I had my own anxieties about life, and I had my own insecurities about myself. I did not understand that the things I grappled with were similar to the things my friends dealt with. I remember sitting in class and thinking that my peers had a better understanding of the lesson. Of course, some of my peers were more engaging with the teacher and were more expressive in their understanding of the lesson. I did not realize, until later on during my junior college years, that we were all basically at the same level of understanding, trying to make meaning of the lesson. Irrespective of what might have caused your insecurity, I ask that you objectively reevaluate and revalue you. You are incredibly special and deserve to be construed as such. Protect yourself!

Self-respect

How does one build self-respect? I would like for you to stand in front of a mirror, look straight in your own eyes and say, "I deeply admire myself!" If you do not have access to a mirror, then close your eyes and repeat that self-affirming statement. Even though building self-esteem takes more than repeating mantras, this is a good first step in rebuilding or enhancing your self-respect. Think, believe, and articulate that you are special. With this positive notion, any self-esteem challenges you face will begin to dissipate, and any negative impressions others have of you will become irrelevant. When you have a healthy self-respect, you will be less likely to be affected by negativity in all its forms, and you will become impervious to circumstances that are geared towards disparaging you. Do not allow your fluctuating emotions to dictate your responses. Emotions were not designed to lead. They are the signals that alert you to potential disturbances in the psychological realm, just as your physical pain alerts you of cause for concern in the physical realm. You may be temporarily distracted by difficult emotions, but it is empowering to own them, and work through them so that they can lead you to a healthier place. Be sure to always check in with yourself, feel your trepidations, experience the anxieties, and prevail. This is an invigorating exercise.

Do not allow your emotion to thrust you into a state of isolation and self-pity, or cause you to become your own agent of self-destruction. Every successful person that I have interviewed, and every life story that I have examined, confirmed that life subjects us to a combination of pleasantness and hardships. Hardship is not necessarily a bad thing. You are positioned to actualize your greatest potential when you face and conquer adversity. Deal with it. If you embrace adversity and overcome it, you will develop the mental fortitude required to continue your journey towards your destiny. Every bad thing that happens to you has the potential to make you stronger. When people say disapproving things to you, unless it is a valid critique worthy of introspection, do not take it personally. It is not about you, it is about them. What people say about you is not your business, it is their business. When you have a high regard for yourself, no external forces will be able to diminish your worth.

If you are invited to a table, engage your intellect. Never come to the table empty-minded. While at the table, if you are convicted of your point of view, hold your position without conceit. Show up with your own perspective and an inquiring mind. Own and defend your opinion. You do not have to think like everybody else. You do not have to change your opinion because it does not align with the status quo. Stand by your conviction and do not equivocate. If it turns out that another point of view is more valid than yours, be honorable enough to submit. Do not surround yourself with those who always agree with you or those who always disagree with you. Surround yourself with people who have their own convictions and opinions. Surround yourself with assertive people who are unafraid to state and own their point of view. Surround yourself with people who will challenge and respect you. You do not have to accept everything that people bring to the table. If their contribution proves to be more rational than yours, agree with them and make the necessary adjustment. You do not have the right to fight people concerning their opinions. State your position, and if there is no compromise, agree to disagree. If you are convinced that your perspective is correct, do not waver in the face of opposition.

People will discredit your reputation to advance their agenda. Do not be demeaned by such atrocity. You were not brought here to advance anyone's program on the shoulders of your demise. Do not try to live your life to please everybody. Do not try to live your life with the motive of making people feel good. Do not nurture anyone's happiness at the expense of your peace of mind. For many years, I went the extra mile to ensure that others were positioned for prosperity. Have you ever lived that way? Are you still living that way? Are you the person who always makes sure that everybody else is alright at your expense? Are you the person who is always volunteering for everything at the expense of your leisure time? Stop! If you consistently bend yourself out of shape to accommodate others, you will eventually lose yourself in the process. Many amazingly empathetic people are left lonely, dejected, and devalued because they have exhausted their emotional equity, physical energy, and financial resources for the purpose of selflessly attending to the welfare of others. Going forward, show the highest respect for, and give the greatest regard to, matters concerning your affairs. Cease and desist from continuously putting the interests of others above yours.

Self-worth

You do not need a lot of friends around you. Chances are that some of your friends are givers, some are takers, and others both givers and takers. I learned the hard way. Your self-worth is not measured by the number of friends you may think you have. Some of the people who you regard as being the closest to you, and who you expect to be there for you when you need them most, are the ones who will not show up. Be careful how willing you are to put your personal agenda on hold for others. One of my mentors once told me that I could not save everybody. If the only thing that causes you to feel good about yourself is going the extra mile for others, then you will always attract people in your life who have a need to be rescued.

If you fall, you better get up. Everyone experiences some degree of failure and some level of disappointment. Your successes, failures, or limitations in life do not define you. Individuals who think very poorly of themselves tend to judge themselves and others harshly. Some may even seek to elevate themselves by putting others down. If they can stand on your head and hold you to the ground, it makes them temporarily feel better about themselves. Stay away from such individuals because their energy has the potential to weigh you down. Conversely, when credible people find themselves in the gutter, be willing to go down there and assist in pulling them out. If your self-worth is wholesome, you will have no apprehension in reaching down and pulling someone from a desolate place. You should not be afraid to be associated with the downtrodden. I have had the experience of reaching down and helping others rise from the debris of life's depravities, only to be faced with criticism from observers who misjudged my intention. I am resolved to continue helping the downtrodden, and I am not afraid of critical reviews. Let nothing deter you from uplifting others, irrespective of the potentially upsetting repercussions. What are you trying to preserve by avoiding the disrepute? What or who are you trying to protect? Are you trying to protect your reputation? You should be more concerned about protecting your character than your reputation. You will enhance your character as you seek to enhance the worth of the unfortunate. We all have mountains and valleys to navigate. We all have encounters that we would rather not have to deal with. Consequently, we should all be empathetic towards others. Your limitation may differ from that of the other person, but it does not mean that you are a better or worse human being. Who are we to judge anyone?

My father was not a rich man, but he was a positively proud man who highly valued himself. He had 6 children and if you have met any of us, you would have seen the mark of self-worth emanating from all of us. We do not allow people to push us around and I attribute that to the way our father molded us. It does not matter the level of your social status; my father would be respectful if you earned it and he would reprimand you with the same fervor if you violated him. He said that if he was wearing your garments and you disrespect him, he would not be hesitant to put you in your place. Stand your ground and do not allow the actions of others to diminish your personhood.

You will experience some good days, and you will also experience some bad days. You will have ups, and you will have downs. Your self-worth is not determined by the quality of your day nor by the intensity of your fortune or misfortune. It comes from how you handle the things that are thrown at you from every angle on any given day. You have tremendous potential, and you should focus your attention on realizing it. Aspire to be your best self. Do not focus on how you are being evaluated by others. If you believe that you are good enough to take on a challenge in life, then forge ahead with that positive outlook. You are as good a human being as anyone else. You are a promise and a possibility. You are endowed with a great, big bundle of potentiality. No one is better than you are. You can only sleep in one bed at any given time, just like everyone else. You can only wear one pair of shoes at any given time, just like everyone else. Whether you must take public transportation or ride in a Lamborghini, you stand an equal chance of eventually getting to your destination.

Material things should never define the caliber of person you distinguish yourself to be. First be defined by the fact that you are a human being. You are a child of the universe, and you have a right to be here. The bottom line is that you have just as much rights as anyone to occupy your space on the face of the earth and fulfil the mission you are placed here to accomplish. No single human being is superior to you. Value and assert yourself as a person who is as important as anyone else. Irrespective of genetic code, your material acquisition, or your social status, you have the right to be here and a mandate to make your mark. Embrace your self-worth and refuse to agitate yourself to meet anyone's expectation or to be a part of any clique.

I have had some great experiences in life, and I have also had some horrible ones. When my back was against the wall, when everything around me seemed as if they were going downhill, and it seemed as though everything I built in life was about to be demolished, I remained stubbornly hopeful. I am still not sure of how I survived and conquered so much turmoil, and maintained a healthy mind, body, and spirit. I am thankful that I did not allow myself to be devastated by the years of adversities that life imposed upon me. When you value yourself, your healthy self-worth will cause you to be a conqueror, and whatever happens around you will not be able to compromise the fortitude and strength of purpose that is established within you. Your outlook will remain positive, even though your adversities may seek to redefine your scenario differently. Know who you are. You are the embodiment of greatness. Pause and tell yourself that you are indeed the embodiment of greatness.

You are special. You are the standard-bearer for your unique journey, from birth, throughout life, and until the end of your time on earth. Let nothing cause you to question this resolve. You will have your moments of disruption but patiently work through them and choose to enjoy a peaceful existence. Refuse to cultivate or entertain negative energy, instead use your energy to strengthen your determination to overcome your distractions, bolster your spirit, enhance your mental health, and excel in every aspect of your life. When adversity comes, respond with optimism and a resolution to overcome. Your emotional intelligence and mental stability should be such that when negative things occur in your life, you will entertain no other option except the expectation of an eventual outcome that will lead to your betterment. You may not always be as strong as you desire, but be consummately determined to foster the will to overcome. A winning mentality, positive outlook, well maintained body, and nurtured spiritual life, is a recipe for success. When pressures confront you, respond with confidence and prevail!

Points to Ponder

    a. Believe in yourself

        i. See yourself as an ideal human being

        ii. Highly regard your innate and acquired virtues

        iii. Define yourself by your virtues and not by how others perceive you

    b. Trust your convictions

        i. If you truly believe that something is right for you, then refuse to waver

        ii. If you truly believe that something is right for you, then fully embrace it

        iii. If you truly believe that something is right for you, then be settled in your mind

    c. Stand your ground

        i. Always come to the table with your own set of ideals

        ii. Stand by your core values in the face of disapproval

        iii. Never devalue your point of view if you are convinced of its relevance

    d. Get over people

        i. Never be deterred by the negative perceptions of others

        ii. Never be dissuaded by the subjective judgment of others

   iii. Never dwell on rejections

  e. Set and maintain clearly defined boundaries

    i. Establish how you want your attention, energy, and time to be used

   ii. Let it be known when your attention, energy, and time are violated

  iii. Be remorseless in discarding violators of your attention, energy, and time

Nothing is more mentally tumultuous than being compelled to disassociate from a situation that captures the heart and entangles the emotion; however, whenever the need arises, you must harness the courage and take every necessary step to maintain your dignity.

Reflections

_____

_____

_____

_____

_____

_____

_____

_____

_____

_____

_____

_____

_____

_____

_____

_____

_____

Chapter 3

Stop Expecting
Your Expectations Of Others Have No Guarantees

— ★ ★ ★ —

If you expect others to make room for your growth, then you are operating on risky grounds because some people will, and others will not. The credibility of your perceptions and decisions could be radically compromised by your assumptions. The universe takes care of those who align themselves with their self-generated positivity and good intentions.

Expectations

I am getting ready to delve into a subject that will either make or break your ability to navigate life effectively. It is something that, with great effort and learning, I have tried to manage in my life. The subject is *Expectations*. Your peace of mind and ability to navigate life's challenges are tied to how well you manage your expectations. So, what is expectation? I will not reference a dictionary. I am coming to you from the school of hard knocks; from having been on the earth for a long time, from having to deal with people, and mostly from having to deal with myself. A good friend of mine was dealing with some challenges and I ensured that I provided consistent moral support until the matter was resolved. Shortly after this scenario, I was faced with a very life-altering situation and anticipated that my friend would reciprocate the support. That never happened. It was a painful experience for me. Maybe the friend did not have the capacity to support me at that time; however, it left me feeling disappointed in my friend and it also diminished the level of confidence that I had in this particular friendship.

You may think that you have it all together, but you can be caught off guard at any given time. At some point in time in your life, you will be faced with unanticipated occurrences. Sometimes your response to a stimulus will surprise even you. You might have taken on a simple assignment that you thought could be easily handled but found out that it developed into a problematic challenge. When I was a fired-up youngster, I asserted that I could be in the same room with the 'devil,' and it would not negatively impact me because I had the ability to remain focused and disaffected. After maturing and entering the marketplace, I realized that I would rather not be in the same room with the 'devil' because the evolution of unpredictable outcomes could distort my expectation and complicate my very existence.

Expectation is an assumption or a set of assumptions that we embrace as we engage in life's interactions. We tend to enter every interaction with a set of assumptions. The credibility of our perceptions and the impact of our decisions will be shaped by our expectations. There are basically two types of expectations; the ones that are expressed and those that are unexpressed. I found that whenever I facilitate premarital counseling, the couples are usually willing to articulate the expectations with which they are comfortable. However, there is always another set of unexpressed expectations below the surface. A couple is usually reluctant to bring these hidden expectations to the table. I discover that oftentimes the parties have conflicting unexpressed expectations, and it is not apparent to either party that these counteracting points of views existed. Bringing these expectations to light, and requiring that they be discussed, will invariably elevate the conversation to a level that could either be amicable or cantankerous. Expressing these expectations often result in surprises for both parties. It will; however, lead to insights which will preempt future conflict and potentially provide clarity and resolution.

Assumptions

It is the set of assumptions that we bring into our interactions that establishes expectations. You may have friends with whom you are building social relationships, or you may be courting with the intention of establishing an intimate relationship. You may accept a job thinking that your zeal and academic qualifications will be enough to sustain your interest and longevity. I served in the public school system as an educator for almost 25 years. When I did my first interview for employment in the public school system, I remember quite vividly telling the interviewers that I loved children and wanted to make sure that I deposited in them positive virtues that they would eventually take with them into the marketplace and excel in their fields of interest. I assumed that I possessed the innate ability to manage my classroom environment and that my students would be receptive to my pedagogical approach. My early days as an educator were so challenging that I began to question whether I had made the correct career choice. I assumed that it would be smooth sailing from the outset but I was disappointed. My zeal and educational philosophy could hardly sustain me during my early days as a classroom teacher. As a beginner, I remember constantly calling the principal's office whenever my students became disruptive. I assumed that a call to the principal's office, or an occasional visit from the principal or security officer, would intimidate my students to comply with my directives. A visit from the principal or security officer provided only a temporary reprieve. After a while the principal refused to respond to my calls. One day he indicated to me that, whenever I called for help, I was undermining my own authority and ability to effectively manage my classroom. That was the last day I called the principal's office for classroom management assistance. I quickly improved my classroom management skills and instructional delivery strategies. This change in assumption resulted in an improved classroom climate and culture.

I remember taking a vacation to the Dominican Republic with my two children some years ago. I booked a resort, which looked incredibly beautiful and accommodating in the virtual tour and brochure. When we arrived at the destination, we were impressed. Our impression remained intact until we were escorted to our room. To our dismay, the room was not habitable. It was unkempt and the furniture dilapidated. I remember my son becoming extremely upset after trying hard, for a very short time, to conceal his disappointment. He was outraged at the resort management. Surprisingly, he was also outraged at me. He was about nine years old at that time. I called the resort management and informed them that we would not be staying in that room because the appearance was not consistent with the picture that the virtual tour painted. We were eventually relocated to a much better room.

Another area in which you can have unmet expectations is within specialized communities. You become a part of a community, and you have an expectation of becoming integrated into a community of plausible individuals. You expect that the members of the community are aspiring to build common values based on a common philosophy. You expect that the culture of the community will reflect unconditional love, tolerance, and support. As you become more embedded within the community's culture you may discover that some of the people have competing, and even conflicting values and approaches to life. In this community, you may encounter people at varying levels of maturity, mindfulness, and awareness. They also may have varying levels of emotional intelligence. I once joined an organization that prided itself in being the standard bearer for brotherhood, unity, and spirituality. It did not take me long to discover that these relationships were primarily transactional. Your endorsement would be guaranteed only if you aligned yourself with the subjective views of the masses within the group. I discovered quite early that if your views were different, irrespective of how rational they were, you would be ostracized and labelled as a disrupter of the culture. When you discover that your expectations are not met within a particular community, you can become despondent and isolated. Luckily for me, I learned that I should not attach my happiness or self-worth to the approval of others. If you adopt this position, then I can assure you that your peace of mind would be protected.

Do not assume that people are going to reciprocate your care, and that the system for which you have loyally and sacrificially served is going to reward you in equal measure. You raise your children and you expect that they will be accessible to you whenever you desperately need them. You have the expectation that, because you sacrificed your life and cared so much for them from childhood to adulthood, they are going to be there for you. There are no guarantees with this expectation. I have two kind and compassionate children; however, I will not plan my life around their availability when I get to the stage where I need assisted living. I am making independent provisions. I do believe my children will be there for me but I am not planning around that expectation.

Disappointments

At some point in your life, you should step back and reconfigure your philosophy concerning matters of the heart, such as the handling of disappointments. I will guarantee you that disappointments are inevitable. The way you respond to your disappointments is based on how much you are invested in the situation. If you approach situations without objectivity, you will sometimes miss blatant red flags and inadvertently get drawn into unsurmountable dysfunctionalities. Pay attention, or else you could be setting yourself up for unintended emotional trauma and chaos of some sort. You have to engage in situations with an understanding that they may not work out exactly the way you had predicted. I am not coming to you with negativity because I am not a negative person. I am very positive in my outlook and I am also realistic. This should be the proactive approach that we all take when determining our involvements. I was once asked to make a presentation, and I was unable to deliver all the content, so I gave my notes to the host of the event and suggested that the remainder of the content be presented at a subsequent convenient time. I later learned that the host was offended by the suggestion. I found this response perplexing, and must confess that it actually left me feeling disconsolate for a while. I did not allow this negative emotion to linger. I took consolation in the fact that my motive was pure. Be very purposeful in guarding your emotions because they are much more fragile than you probably envision.

I have always considered myself to be an amazingly strong individual. I am also perceived in that manner by those who know me well, especially my immediate family members and close associates. I consider myself an even keel person, and I understand that every one of us is vulnerable to some degree of emotional fragility. If you keep believing in people, investing in them, embracing them, and giving them unconditional trust, then you will become vulnerable to disappointments and emotional upheavals. Trust is a double-edged sword. As I matured, I decided to take an approach that I would initially give everyone 100% trust and adjust the degree of trust based on how people demonstrated their trustworthiness. I realized quite early that such an approach carried with it some risks and needed some rethinking. My disappointments were frequent and impactful and I was inclined to take the stand of sequestering myself from people. Therapists would call this a classic "trauma response" and trauma responses are maladaptive ways of creating safety in our connections. Disappointment and pain cannot be avoided in human relationships but resorting to skepticism can limit true intimacy, friendship, depth, and ultimately meaningful human connection. Rather than avoiding disappointment, it is best to determine what lessons we learn about ourselves and others through disappointment. The healthier approach here is to increase your emotional capacity for dealing with the pain of disappointments and not avoiding deep connections in an effort to avoid disappointment altogether.

Entrepreneurs pursue business opportunities for their own benefit and not for the benefit of their employees. They do not plan their growth strategies with a desire to make employees rich. Entrepreneurs start businesses so that they can accumulate wealth for themselves and their families. Employees are primarily a factor of production in that process, and will be given incentives to motivate them towards efficiency, but they are never the main priority. As a valued employee, you can tangibly contribute to the success of your employer's business, but you have to understand that you are only valued to the extent that your ability meets the expectations of the bottom-line. If you do not understand your role in any organization or social setting, then when the inevitable disappointments come, you will be caught off guard. If you are a part of an organization and it is evident that your value has been diminished to the point where you are dispensable, become proactive and put into effect your exit plan and do not wait for the disappointment of a termination notice. Reinvent yourself and create new growth opportunities.

You might have invested your trust and time in individuals you considered your friends and associates. You might be involved with people who you assume will protect your interest in the event that the need arises. When you are faced with a crisis and need support, you will get a better picture of who are your genuine friends and associates. As the adage goes, *'The proof of the pudding is in the eating'*. The type and amount of support you need in a crisis is dependent upon the nature of the crisis. You may only need someone to put a hand on your shoulder or words of comfort and encouragement. The people in whom you have invested your time, or for whom you have sacrificed your resources, could become your greatest source of disappointment at a time when you most desire their support. That could be the case because such individuals do not have the same degree of investment in your welfare as you have in theirs. They might not even have that same measure of appreciation, or capacity, for the relationship as you have demonstrated. Their friendship value system might not be wired the same way as yours. We should be careful not to rate other people's response to our needs based on the degree of our attentiveness to them in their times of need. Some people may truly care about you, but demonstrate their care for you in a manner that does not necessarily match the intensity of your care towards them.

You might be inclined to be resentful of others because they never came through for you, especially when you needed them most. To avoid this, I want you to go back to the drawing table and make sure that you revisit and reassess your relationships and expectations. Your empathic nature could subject you to disappointing responses from the people you least expect. There are individuals who will establish relationships with you on a transactional basis. They target you to meet specific needs and will remain loyal to you for as long as the need exists and you are delivering the resources. Nothing will bring to light the integrity of a person more than the way they treat you after the need has been met. This is one reality of life that usually becomes apparent to you after the fact, so remain vigilant whenever you allow new acquaintances in your space.

Emotional Equity

Those of you who are planning on establishing relationships should cautiously and measuredly give of your emotional equity. Your emotional equity is like an investment portfolio. As you allocate your emotional capital, unless you are receiving returns on your investments, you are depleting your emotional account and compromising its value. If your account is not replenished, and there are no deposits, then eventually you will go bankrupt. That will likely happen when your relationship non-negotiables are not properly established and managed. Many people are left emotionally impoverished to the extent that they are unable to function in a normal manner. They utilized their emotional equity in accommodating others, without the assurance of any reinvestment in their lives. If this has become your reality, then you are heading for an emotional catastrophe. This leads to an emptiness that can be crippling. Please understand that when you operate on empty, you are actually on a self-destructive path, and this will lead to a feeling of dejection. Your self-esteem will be negatively impacted, and your creative juices will be dried up. It is very important that you stop depositing in the lives of people who do not possess the integrity, willingness or common decency to show regard for your kindness. .

If you live in a place where you are having all kinds of recurring hurtful episodes in your life, then it is time for you to examine yourself and see whether your empathy is working against you. Could it be that you are disproportionately investing your emotional equity in the welfare of others. Could it be that your excessive investment in those around you is taking away from your ability to focus more on yourself? Nothing is wrong with endowing others, but this should not be done at the expense of your personal wellbeing, and neither should it be done for recompense. If you expect that your acts of benevolence will always be reciprocated, then you are setting up yourself to be disappointed. If you are engaged in an altruistic gesture and expect a particular outcome, you must embrace the possibility that your expectations may not be realized. Regulate your acts of kindness and focus more on attending to your own needs. You might think this is an egocentric stance, but wisdom will teach you the virtue of prioritizing your personal necessities. I resolve not to do things because I expect something in return. I do acts of goodwill because they are aligned with my values, or simply because I feel compelled to do so. I really do not have much expectation of payback. If we approach life with this mentality, then we will experience fewer disappointments and heartaches.

Motives

You may do things because you want to impress others, gain friendships, or to obtain accolades. If that is the case then you are taking a disingenuous approach to life. Counteract this unimpressive approach by improving your self-esteem to the point where you do not crave affirmation, praise or approval from others. Affirmation can be a good thing, but whenever others acknowledge you for what you have done, do not dwell there and do not build a monument to memorialize it. There is a difference between affirmation and approval. Affirmation is declaring something to be true. Approval is accepting or allowing something, or extending a complimentary reception. You do not need another person's declaration of your truth to own it. Do not wait for anyone to extend anything to you or offer you a compliment in order to embrace your creativity and actualize your potential.

You are the originator and architect of your dreams and aspirations. The anticipation of people's discontentment with your wishes has the potential to distract and ultimately devastate you. There is no requirement that you have to be approved, appreciated, or loved by the masses. If someone approves of you, accept it with no fanfare; and if someone disapproves of you, let it be a nonissue for you. Whether someone appreciates you or demonstrates a lack of appreciation towards you, remain focused on what you set out to accomplish. If you live with the expectancy of endorsement, then your focus is misdirected. Generally, people will approve of you, engage you, and think well of you, if you are aligned with their agenda. Always remember that everyone comes to the table with an agenda. People's reactions are generally not about you; they are about their own motivations.

If management promotes you to a senior position, you will more than likely see surprising changes in the behaviors of your former peers on the job. If your attitude remains consistent, and you retain the spirit of collegiality, your former peers will still have issues with you. People are satisfied with you as long as you are not elevated above their level in certain aspects of life. If you accomplished your desired level of upward mobility, the same people who cheered you on along the way may later on disapprove of you. Do not expect that your social circle will remain undisrupted as you climb the success ladder. You do not have to act inappropriately to be resented or disliked. You do not have to deliberately offend anyone to be treated with abhorrence. If you expect that everybody wants the best for you, you will be disappointed. If you keep your motivations pure and avoid the need for praise, then you are definitely not destined for disillusionment.

Your success can become a threat to those around you. That is where the human condition of covetousness comes into play. A friend of mine once told me that you could give all of your resources to a covetous person, and that person would continue being covetous towards you. You could give that individual all your possessions, and resentment would still be harbored towards you. Covetousness is a spirit. It is a mental and spiritual dysfunction. It is a destructive attitude. Do you know of anyone who dislikes you for no apparent reason? When people have resolved to be malicious towards you, there is hardly anything you can do to change their motivations. You never deliberately offended them, and you have always been amicable towards them, yet they begrudge you. You have to understand that society is not a level playing field. If you do not understand that there are people who wish for your demise, you are in for a lifetime of unpleasant surprises. Do not take anything at face value. As the old adage indicates, *'Not all that glitters is gold.'* Allow adequate time for true motivations to be exposed. Never be deterred by unwarranted offences.

Here is how I am recommending that you move forward. Step out in life and be the best version of yourself. Make sure that your motives are good. It is impossible to avoid disappointment because people's motives will not always be in sync with yours. We can prepare ourselves to deal with the pain of disappointment by realizing that people can fall short of our expectations. Your mantra should be that if people fall short of our expectation, then instead of agitating over it, we should prepare to find a viable alternative. Absolutely no one cares about your passion as much as you care about it. Step out into the world with a desire to do well and do not rely on the effort of others to accomplish your goals. Do not allow negative energy to compromise your value system and your ability to make your dreams come true. Continue to be altruistic. Continue to be caring. Despite your disappointment in some individuals, continue to think well of others. If you do good, have the right attitude, and take the right approach to life, you will be elevated to heights you never dreamt you could attain. What you sow, that will you reap.

Discernment

My personal interactions are informed by one of my philosophies, '*I am more impressed with a heart-shake than a handshake.*' People can approach you and shake your hand enthusiastically, while in their hearts they do not wish you well. It is the energy that emanates from the heart that matters. You have to get in touch with your own intuition, look beyond people's actions, and perceive the quality of the energy that they are emanating. We should be careful not to become paranoid about everyone's intentions. Instead, we should become conversant in listening to our intuition and be proficient in evaluating the tenor of those with whom we interact. This will position us to gain valuable insights that will shape our reactions and interpersonal dynamics.

In order to align you with their personal agenda, people will analyze and tell what they surmise you want to hear. Be careful how you allow flattery to impact your response. Based on my many years of interaction with people, I have developed a fairly good understanding of human behavior; however, there is always the uncertainty of human unpredictability. If there is one social skill that you need to refine, it is the skill of discernment. This does not entail going to your bed and getting a dream or have a feeling about a situation based on your own insecurities. It is about listening to your heart and trusting what it is saying to you. There may be times when you have to shut out the noise, dig deep, listen intently, and learn to make meaning of what your inner voice is communicating to you. Your ability to see beyond face value, and grasp the bigger picture of hidden agendas, is a determining factor in securing your clarity of mind. Be careful how liberal you are with your trust and generosity. It is wise to embrace and believe in others with an alert mind and a perceptive spirit. The more you blindly embrace, the more potentially devastating your inevitable disappointments will be. Take nothing for granted.

Whether you are operating in the corporate or religious worlds, or within the realms of family and friendship, tread both cautiously and assertively. Walk through life with your guard up and your blinders off. I have learned that this is the safest approach in navigating the minefields of the personal or professional worlds. I started out in life zealous to enter the world and collaborate amicably with my fellow human beings. During my formative years, I thought that the world was a level playing field and that all people were just so amazingly wonderful, good-natured, and have the best regards for their fellow human beings. Unfortunately, that has not always been the case. My perspective on life has evolved as I grew up fast and faced many adversities. Where am I in life now? One, I believe in me. Two, I align my lifestyle with my values, standards and interests. Three, my expectations are based on the outcomes of my own effort and aspirations.

We have the capability to be the best or the worst version of ourselves. Positive and negative peer pressure impact both children and adults. Many people will walk with you, but if it comes down to making a sacrificial choice, they will make it in their own interest, and sometimes even at your expense, without remorse or timidity. If it requires that they change direction and leave you deserted, they most likely will. A smile should not necessarily be taken as a sign of friendship or community. A handshake should not necessarily be taken for loyalty or commitment. An embrace should not necessarily be taken for a feeling of affection. Make sure that you are always in touch with yourself and in touch with your inner voice. Trust your intuition. Coupled with your values, your instincts are like a GPS system, helping you to navigate human complexities. Learn to listen and hear what has not been verbalized. You can sometimes gain more insights from what has been left unsaid. Listen, evaluate, and respond with precision.

Surround yourself with those who have proven over time that they genuinely mean you well, but still keep in mind that people are susceptible to change. Love unconditionally and, at the same time, please note that some who seek out your company and display positivity towards you, can be the same persons who, in your absence, smear you or remain silent when others disparage you. Be careful who you trust with your innermost feelings, because if such an individual breaches your confidence, the deceit could erode your ability to trust and also take a toll on your mental health. If you live by these principles, you will be less surprised or negatively impacted by acts of deception. These are matters of the heart that should be frequently contemplated. You can easily identify people who have been to the school of hard knocks, and people who have had their significant share of disenchantments. They live cautiously and establish boundaries. They are assertive and not easily impressed by anyone. Take note, you should be about aligning with your values, rather than trying to please others. Secure and maintain your own happiness rather than catering to the happiness of others. Be good to yourself and, to the best of your ability, to others. If you adhere to these pragmatic principles, you will experience an empowering, enlightening, and fulfilled life. My grandmother, Albertha Baimbridge, died at the age ninety-five. She was an independent single mother who raised my mother and two sons. She owned her home and took care of her affairs for the duration of her active years. She spoke her mind, and did not allow anyone to take advantage of her. She commanded respect and lived on her own terms. From all indications, she lived a great life. I am hoping to emulate her in this regard. Seek to live your best life now!

Points to Ponder

   a. Approach every situation with a clean slate

      i. Rid yourself of preconceived ideas before addressing situations

     ii. Be objective in your approach

    iii. Be sure not to predetermine the outcome

   b. Listen more and speak less

      i. Be slow to speak

     ii. Spend more time listening than speaking

    iii. Listen attentively to all perspectives and points of views with objectivity

   c. Hear what is not being expressed

      i. Pay attention to body language and insinuations

     ii. Observe unspoken messages and interpret the messages sent by body language

    iii. Revaluate, check for clarification, and reframe, based on observation

   d. Ascertain a clear understanding of every engagement

      i. Never come to conclusions based on the unexpressed thoughts of others

   ii.   Let others explain their thinking instead of presuming what they meant

  iii.   Do not refute the explanation given by others concerning their thoughts

e.   Ensure that emotional engagements are reciprocal and equitable

    i.   Be tentative and measured in your emotional engagement

   ii.   Give only as much as you receive in emotional engagements

  iii.   Never build alliance with the emotionally disengaged or emotionally unavailable

Emotional availability is central to the establishment and sustainability of an amicable relationship. The absence of this ingredient from any relationship is a recipe for an exercise in futility and despair; disengage promptly and move on.

Reflections

_____

_____

_____

_____

_____

_____

_____

_____

_____

_____

_____

_____

_____

_____

_____

_____

_____

_____

Chapter 4

The "ME" in the Matter

What Is In It For Me?

★ ★ ★

In certain instances you can make amends, but it is impossible to do anything about the misgivings of your past. Your past is history so do not allow yourself to be anchored to it. Start living your best life today, free from the stigmas of yesterday.

Me

We may spend an inordinate amount of our time supporting people, making sure that their welfare is taken care of, and making sure that we assist them in getting on the right path. Somewhere along the way, we often give too much of ourselves, our energy, our emotional capacity, our intellectual capital, and our attention. People deliberately or inadvertently exploit us; some take from us and to others we give of ourselves voluntarily. Some beneficiaries of our altruism exercise discretion while others manipulate us. Others are relentless in taking more and more of both our tangible and intangible resources.

In my own life, for many years, I kept giving generously of myself. However, when I got to a place where I needed support, there was little to be found. I have come to realize that supporting others in their times of need does not guarantee that I will be supported by them in my time of need. When it is our turn to be supported, many of us who give of ourselves can be hard pressed to find people who are willing to show up for us and help us in overcoming our circumstances. I am not saying this because I am a complainer. I am saying this because I am a realist. I have had major challenges in my life where I waited expectantly for those who I poured into to at least put a hand on my shoulder or offer words of consolation. Instead, I was left alone to fend for myself. I had to take a look in the mirror, turn the searchlight directly on the inner recesses of my heart and ask, "Where is the 'ME' in the matter?"

In the broader society, rugged individualism is the dominant philosophy. I grew up in a religious culture where I was socialized to prioritize serving others. There is a religious code that implores us to love our neighbor as ourselves. However, it does not indicate that we should love our neighbor more than we love ourselves. We oftentimes become so selfless that we incessantly serve others and neglect serving ourselves. Where is the 'ME' in the matter? It is important for us to be unselfish, but we must also learn how to pay attention to ourselves, our needs, and our desires. We should be generous in our service to humanity. This is not only a good principle to embrace, but it is also necessary for our collective survival. We should make a positive contribution to the lives of others, and we should seek to leave the world a better place than we found it. The mark that we make on society might not be archived in a journal or written in a book, but that does not render our contribution insignificant. I am sure that there are many people who died and whose contributions are not recorded in historical records, yet during their lifetime, they impacted those who came under their sphere of influence. It is consoling to know that the impact of such unsung heroes' legacy is written in the lives of those who they positively impacted during their lifetime.

At the writing of this book, I have been a public school educator for close to 25 years. I served in the American public school system as a teacher, guidance counselor, high school vice-principal, and district-wide administrator. I know the sacrifice that educators have made throughout their careers. Many invested in the lives of students who became notable and productive citizens, some assuming high-profile civic responsibilities. These students made positive contributions to society long after their teachers advanced in age, retired from public service, and passed on from this life. It is consoling to know that the labor of these unsung heroes was positively manifested in the lives of their former students. Unfortunately, following retirement, many educators are faced with immeasurable challenges ranging from lack of financial security, inadequate health care, and even isolation. They sacrificed their lives to serve generations of children, and yet they are left to fend for themselves during one of the most vulnerable stages of their lives. We are admonished to give back to society and contribute to the lives of those around us. However, where we often miss the mark is in securing our own well-being. The kindest of us have the tendency to serve others well and neglect to give priority to our own welfare. We fail to acknowledge and cater to the 'ME' in the matter.

Self-Neglect

One matter that I would like to address is how we tend to neglect ourselves in the process of catering to those around us. There are many individuals who have made positive deposits in others' lives without reciprocation, and subsequently become depleted to the point where they experience cognitive chaos. This is a state of mind that manifests itself in demotivation, depression, disillusionment, and disarray. This condition could lead to a depletion of mental energy and a feeling of abandonment. The kindest, most giving, and most empathic people are predisposed to cognitive chaos.

Many self-sacrificing individuals are locked up in the solitary confinement of their homes with tears on their pillow and pain in their heart. They get up each day and from all external indicators they seem to enjoy a satisfying existence. They are able to function efficiently in the public arena, but deep down on the inside, they are feeling empty, unfulfilled and unhappy. Their contentment is diminished, and their social life is uninteresting at best and non-existent at worst. They may even interact with myriads of people on a daily basis, but feel like they have no one who can relate to their conundrum. If not addressed, this scenario leads to depression. Depression can be a result of the perception of isolation, and often times it is an inaccurate assessment. Such individuals may not have others in their lives with the perception and sensitivity to identify the disturbing emotional red flags, or who will step up to the plate and engage them in meaningful social interactions. They have no one with the intuition or initiative to invite them for a walk in the park or a time of fun in a refreshing social setting. So, they superficially interact with people around them, and everyone looks on and thinks that they are happy and that all is well with them. The people around them do not understand that when these undetected unfulfilled persons retreat to the confines of their isolation at home then the hurting heart, the unmet desires, the depressive mood, the social distancing, and the loneliness, have become the self-destructive norm for them. Do you, or individuals that you know of, fit this description in any form or fashion?

I have had my own bouts of depression. I have had my own bouts of isolation and all the trappings that are associated with it. I have been down this desolate path of pain and panic. Have you ever been there? Are you there now? We have a tendency to look with admiration on those who are influencers and assume that they have it all together, not realizing that they are sometimes the ones with the most trying circumstances. If you keep allowing substantial withdrawals from your emotional equity without obtaining replenishments, then after a while, you lose yourself and your ability to find meaning in life. This devastating disposition will one day compel its victims to check on the status of their existence, and hopefully they will come to terms with the brutal fact that they have neglected themselves. The challenge is that when they eventually make this self-discovery, there will be an overwhelming amount of self-work that needs to be done in order to get on track for meaningful life. This outcome is not necessarily true for every empathetic person. Self-abandonment is not in itself endemic to empathy, it is a trauma response rooted in maladaptive beliefs about what creates worth and meaning in life. So, you have to take a calculated approach in establishing the delicate balance between altruism and self-loyalty. They are not mutually exclusive; they both can occur concurrently. To a great extent you have control over the present and your future occurrences in your life, but you have no control over the past. Despite this fact, you can learn from the past and use it as a guide to help you to make informed decisions for the present and the future. The encouraging news is that from this point forward, you can purposefully develop an attainable goal-oriented strategic plan that is geared towards a lifestyle that focuses on taking care of yourself, one that focuses on the 'ME' in the matter.

Priority

You can lose your lease on life if you allow yourself to be caught in a perpetual cycle of prioritizing the needs of others over your personal needs. Get comfortable with making yourself the number one priority. Be helpful towards others, but it is imperative that the stewardship of our own existence remains your number one priority. This approach to life is necessary because if you are able to securely stand on your own footing, you will be able to sustain yourself and those you desire to assist. First aspire to stand on solid ground before you delve into the affairs of others. This mode of operation should be adhered to in all types of relationships, whether they be personal, family, or professional. There should be no exception to the rule. If you are involved in an intimate relationship and your partner is not pulling the reasonably expected weight, you need to reevaluate the relationship and make the necessary adjustment in your best interest. If you do not make a change in your interest then the inequity will perpetuate. Does this resonate with you?

People have the power and prerogative to change their undesirable circumstances, even though it is more daunting for some. If you are overly concerned about how your adjustment might impact the dynamics of your interpersonal relationships and your other associations, then you might resort to inaction. This could lead to your own detriment. Focus on the 'ME' in the matter. Make whatever reasonable adjustments necessary to refocus on yourself and enhance the quality of your life. You need nobody's approval to empower yourself. Become reacquainted with yourself and practice to be happy all by yourself. Take a walk all by yourself on the boardwalk, in the park or by the river, and reflect on the manner in which you are leading your life. Become exhilarated by doing nature walks by yourself. Go to a restaurant of your choice, suspend your diet for the evening, and treat yourself to a scrumptious meal. While you are doing so, learn to enjoy your own company. It is best to take these reflection expeditions without company, especially when engaging in exercises designed for personal introspection and self-evaluation. Engaging in this exercise by yourself will avoid unnecessary disruptions, distractions or infringements. When applicable, it would be great to actually include a meditation or mindfulness exercise, such as journaling or deep breathing, to help you connect with your needs; or in a nonjudgmental manner reflect on ways you might be neglecting yourself. These are sacred moments that can result in the enrichment of the mind and spirit.

Do not become dependent on others when searching for solace because by so doing, you could find yourself in an unfortunate cycle of unhealthy codependency. If the fear of being alone or neglected overwhelms you, then you are at risk of compromising your peace of mind for shallow companionship. You could actually lose your identity as you grapple with maintaining shallow relationships, especially if they are inclined to be toxic. Never seek to resuscitate a noxious affiliation for the sake of companionship. Exerting consistent effort to maintain a relationship with an inconsistent friend is harmful to your personal wellbeing. You could very well be only construed as a convenient source of support. Do not allow others to engage you as a resource to meet their personal needs. Make it a habit to take inventory of your interpersonal associations. Follow your premonition and do not for a moment believe that everyone who engages you has your best interest at heart. Some connections are transactional, and they will remain intact as long as you honor your end of the transaction, which is often the weightier end. You must learn to say enough is enough and move on.

I have a recommendation that I would like you to adhere to going forward and for the rest of your life. Update the plans for your life by focusing on the 'Me' in the matter. Make yourself the number one priority. Do some amazing things for yourself. Make a deposit in your self-interest and occasionally spend lavishly on something personal of your liking. Take regular vacations. If you lack a good traveling partner, then take a vacation all by yourself. Change that old car that causes you to make innumerable visits to the auto mechanic shop and purchase yourself the dream car while you are still strong enough to enjoy the ride. Increase your discretionary spending by cutting back on some of your financial obligations towards those who have become unreasonably dependent on your generosity. Promptly stop enabling those who take advantage of your kindness. Do not make yourself the solution to people's problems and use your time and resources to take care of your personal needs.

When addressing your personal affairs, it is sometimes necessary that you become blatantly self-centered. If you do not take care of yourself, and life takes a turn for the worst, be assured that some of the people who were recipients of your kindness will be unsympathetic towards you. Many people had amazing dreams and attainable goals but ended up living in the streets. If you get a chance to communicate with some of these homeless people, they will tell you stories about the unfortunate choices that landed them in that predicament. Some homeless people were faced with hard times, and no one stepped up to lend them a helping hand; hence, they were unable to lift themselves from their disastrous circumstances. You have the responsibility to plan your life in a manner that will allow you to work towards your desired outcomes. That is a personal responsibility. It is never too late to revisit your plan and make adjustments. You have limited time to do so because time waits on no one. It is time for you to focus on the 'ME' in the matter.

Points to Ponder

a. Critically review the state of affairs that currently exist in your life

   i. Identify the main people and activities to which you give time and attention

   ii. Determine which people and activities best serve your purpose

   iii. Determine which people and activities least serve your purpose

b. Determine whether you have neglected yourself in your quest for serving others

   i. Clarify whether you make time for others at the expense of your own convenience

   ii. Assess whether you have reserved adequate quality time for leisure

   iii. Confirm whether you prioritize yourself when there is a conflict in the allocation of quality time

c. Ascertain whether you have been settling for the status quo

   i. Recognize the undertakings with which you are no longer comfortable

   ii. Identify the effects that these undertakings are having on your comfort

   iii.   Establish whether you have taken steps to give precedence to your comfort

  d. Adopt an approach that prioritizes you

    i.   Eliminate the undertakings that least meet your personal needs

   ii.   Focus on the undertakings that best meet your personal needs

  iii.   Take frequent uninterrupted leisure time for yourself and engage in self-gratifying activities

  e. Put yourself first

    i.   Say 'no' to all unreasonable infringements on your personal agenda and space

   ii.   Decline or disengage from whatever is destructive to your peace of mind

  iii.   Make yourself the priority

As you effect changes in your life, be sure that you face, own, and reconcile every emotion involved in this transaction. You should do so with the same intensity that you exerted in pursuing and sustaining your new normal of self-enrichment.

Reflections

Chapter 5

FOCUS

Be Selective In Your Focus

— ★ ★ ★ —

Internal freedom constitutes coming to terms with one's authentic self and being at peace with that reality. You should never ignore the promptings of your premonitions. Pay attention!

Pay Attention

You are fortunate if you are breathing and enjoying a measure of health. You are in the land of the living, and you are blessed. I am very much interested in talking about life because I find it very intriguing. I found that some of the things that I talk about from time to time, others would like to talk about them, but they may not have the forum to do so. Others may have a forum, but they might not be willing to express their views because they might be construed as being politically incorrect. Some of the things that I say might not be politically correct, but as long as they are factual, they have the potential to positively impact lives. It is important to note that as you seriously consider the brutal facts of life, your attention will be given to the things that really matter.

Human nature is such that we tend to focus on the wrong things and be distracted from the things that really matter. Some people have a tendency to be judgmental. They look to see the faults and the issues in other people's lives. I have observed that some people tend to preoccupy themselves with what is happening in other people's lives as a distractor from what is happening in their personal lives. So, you find that instead of them spending quality time building on their skills portfolio and learning to efficiently navigate their journey, they preoccupy their valuable time and mind with what is happening in other people's lives. Spending your time preoccupied with other people's issues will distract you from focusing on your own trappings. This distraction may make you feel better about yourself, but it is only a temporary balm. What other people do with their lives is none of your business. You cannot save the world. You are not the messiah. It is important for you to be altruistic. It is important for you to be empathetic. It is important for you to allocate time for meaningful causes and to serve others, but you have to make sure that your motive is appropriate. If you spend your time trying to indulge in other people's lives in an attempt to bolster your own image, then that is not a good approach to life.

I have gained a lot of experience over the years because I have paid attention. I recently told some young men in their teens and early twenties that certain bodies of knowledge will only be acquired as they advance in chronological age. It does not matter how wise and smart they consider themselves to be, the youth will more fully comprehend and appreciate certain facts of life as they advance in age and maturity. It is said that youth is wasted on the young, and I concur, to a certain extent. If I was as wise when I was a youngster, as I am now, I would have avoided certain pitfalls that cost me much. It is said that age is not just a number, and that is a true statement. You should become wiser as you get older. If that is not the case, then you are aging without the expected maturation. If you attempt to climb a flight of stairs after a certain age, you will probably get from the bottom to the top stair successfully, but the task is sometimes a little daunting, especially if you are not consistently engaged in an exercise routine. Grow older gracefully and embrace fully, every stage of your life. Life is about living and dealing with circumstances and dealing with people. This is a challenge; however, you have the ability to adapt to the evolving changes and expectations and enjoy the process to its fullness.

I was giving a presentation where I mentioned that there were certain things in life you would never escape. You will never escape what is destined for you. You cannot evade the inevitable. Whatever constitutes the inevitable, it will be encountered in your life, one way or another. I mentioned the story of a man to whom it was predicted that he would die as a result of an encounter with a cow. He was warned to be very careful, so he sold his farm and purchased the penthouse of an apartment building and decided to reside there for the remainder of his life. He procured the penthouse, and he started living there in an effort to evade the cow encounter. He was determined to alter what was predicted upon his life. He never left the apartment since the day he arrived there. It so happened that on his birthday, they served him a very scrumptious meal specially prepared by a master chef. The chef served him steak for dinner. The man indulged in his meal without reservation. As he started eating the steak, a piece of bone from the steak choked him, and he died. It is likely that this story is fictitious, but it sends a clear message.

The moral of the story is that we cannot escape the inevitable, and therefore, we should not spend our quality time and effort focusing on manipulating things that are aligned with our destiny. There are so many wonderful things that we can focus on in the present time while we anticipate the surfacing of the inescapable impositions of life. We should not allow thoughts of the future to disrupt the prospects of the present. If that man who choked on the bone had enjoyed his life, the sunshine, the rain, the beautiful rivers, and the fresh air, he might have died sooner or later than the time of his death; however, he would have focused on the present and lived a fulfilled life until the time of his demise. In this life, you will face all kinds of episodes but remain focused on the big picture, the journey, and never on the distractions.

Parenting

I have two amazingly brilliant adult children. During their preteen and teenage years, we spent a lot of time together. We took many vacations abroad. During his college years, my son went on a trip to the Bahamas to participate in a musical event. I told him that he was actually on his second trip to the Bahamas. He responded questioningly and indicated that he did not recall his first trip. He wanted to learn more about the first trip because he was so young when we visited the Bahamas on one of our annual father-and-son vacations. I reminded him of when we visited the Bahamas while on a cruise, and I also reminded him of a significant event that occurred on that trip. He remembered the event, but he did not remember that it occurred in the Bahamas. This substantiates the fact that it is the moments that really count. Let us create unforgettable and significant moments and focus less on the mundane and inconsequential.

My son is a fiercely independent young adult, and in his young adult years, he frequently traveled, and mostly alone. There he was in the Bahamas all by himself. He did not remember his first trip, but he remembered what really mattered. He remembered that he went on a cruise with his father and that we stopped on an island. He fondly remembered a situation that remained indelible in his memory. I intentionally created memories for my children. It was a challenge for me to finance those annual vacations. My focus was not on the vacation expenses but on raising my two children and providing them with experiences that would widen their global perspectives and their appreciation for cultural differences.

I learned early in the parenting world that my children were only loaned to me for a very short period. From birth to college years is a very short span of time. Both of my children became painfully independent right after their first year in college. My daughter became a world traveler and expanded her friendship circle. My son discovered the wider world around him and once he acquired his first vehicle, at age 17, our interaction time was significantly reduced. He followed in his sister's footsteps in becoming a frequent flyer. Do not expect your children to fulfill your emotional, social, relational, and other needs. They may love you dearly, but they were only loaned to you. The best you can do is making yourself accessible to them whenever they need you, because parenting is a lifelong vocation.

To those of you who have children, there has got to come a time when you release them and start focusing on your own future. After your children have attained a certain age, your attempt to control them could strain the relationships. Of course, if they need you, then you should be accessible. Motherhood and fatherhood are lifetime assignments, but there needs to be a transition phase when the children are allowed to become responsible for their own journey. I thought that children would just grow up, move out and go on to live their lives ever after. That is not generally the case. Parents constantly think about them. Caring parents are concerned about their children; however, they should not spend their time agitating over the well-being of their children, at the expense of their own sanity and peace of mind. Our children should be given the opportunity to venture out into the world, face the realities of life, make their own mistakes, and grow from their experiences.

Parents, you should not make your grown children's concern and affairs the primary focus of your life. Get a life. You should invest in your children while they are young. You should instill in them the necessary survival skills and model how they are supposed to navigate the rugged terrains of life. Once they get to the stage in life where they begin to fend for themselves, give them space to grow. You should allow your children to become self-actualized. You have to allow your children to chart their own journeys. Do not agitate yourself trying to shield your children from making mistakes. They need to make their own mistakes and learn from them. They will learn from their mistakes if they evaluate them and use them as teachable moments. These are precious moments to be valued and not to be used to judge the integrity of your children's character. Do not spoil these moments by trying to save them from gaining experiences. Do not overindulge in your children's affairs. They will call you when they need you. Focus on yourself.

Middle Age

You should be aware that as you get older, your circle of friends and associates gets smaller, because most of the people with whom you were acquainted from your youthful days are either relocated to other geographical locations, inundated by their own challenging circumstances or have made their transition from the earth. I attended a funeral for one of my colleagues, and I reflected on how he left us at such a relatively young age. He was only in his early 60s. Young people, as you get older, you will fathom that those in their 60s are still relatively young. Trust me, you will surely realize one day. It was consoling to know that those who reflected on my late friend's life indicated that he lived a fulfilled life. I observed that, by their deportment, his children were the products of good parenting. They were mannerly and socially engaging young adults. I also learned that they were doing well for themselves in the marketplace. I was saddened by his passing but I was consoled that my colleague left such a rich legacy behind. I learned from the reflections of his loved ones that my late colleague lived a balanced life. He took frequent vacations and excursions. He was actively engaged in various social endeavors. He enjoyed an active social life. Over three hundred of his family, friends, and associates attended his funeral. It was definitely a consoling and pleasant celebration of life.

Those who reflected on my colleague's life did not make mention of how many assets he accumulated. They did not talk about his various degrees, even though he was a very educated man. They did not talk about his car, although he always drove very prestigious cars. They did not talk about the size and location of his house. Even though he was always impeccably attired, they never talked about the clothes he wore. Everyone talked about the balanced and fulfilled life that this man lived and the lives he positively impacted. He found the key to living optimally. It is important that you fully engage in every aspect of your life because you have an expiration date. You should aspire to live your life in such a manner that you fully exploit every opportunity that is geared towards a satisfying existence. You should focus on enjoying your life. You should make choices that will allow you to embrace a well-rounded lifestyle. Your happiness and peace of mind should be your number one priority. Be sure to focus on yourself, particularly when you approach middle age, because I believe that these should be some of your best days.

Getting Older

From my perspective, life is comprised of four chronological quarters. For those who do not know what quarter of life they are in, I will give you the formula. I consider each 25 years segment of my life as a quarter. If you are 25 years of age or below, then you are living within the first quarter of your life. If you are between 26 and 50 years of age, then you are in the second quarter of your life. If you are between 51 and 75, you are in the third quarter of your life. If you are above 75 years old, you are in the fourth quarter of your life. At this stage of my life, more than ever, I intend to live my best life. I intend to pursue the good things that will lead to fulfilment. I intend to engage in the splendid activities that will inspire me to anxiously look towards the future with excitement. I will pursue the good things that will give me the opportunity to create and innovate. You are never too old to be creative and innovative. Once your health allows you to perform, make full use of every passing day. You can find a new lease on life irrespective of the quarter in which you find yourself. You are not too old to embark on a project, start a new hobby, learn a new skill, or start a new career.

Biblical writings consider King Solomon as the wisest man who ever lived. This wise man Solomon said that we should eat, drink, be merry, and enjoy the partner of our youth. He is saying that in the physical realm, we should focus on taking care of our bodies, our minds, and our relationships. Solomon also implied that it was our duty to nurture our spirituality. I conclude that there are four dimensions of life; the physical, the mental, the spiritual, and the social. Some people focus narrowly on one or the other aspect of these dimensions. If you are focused on the social aspect and are not concerned about the physical, mental, or spiritual aspects, your life is out of equilibrium. You will experience a well-adjusted life only if there is a balance in all four dimensions. This is the balance I propose that we should seek to attain and maintain. You will not enjoy a totally fulfilled life if you are deficient in any of these four dimensions of life. You should intentionally create an atmosphere of positive energy around you; this is fertile ground for you to enjoy a healthy, happy, and rewarding existence. I hope that you will not merrily leave this information in the parking lot, but you will develop a living-well strategic plan around these four dimensions of life.

Mindfulness

As you focus on what really matters in life, there are some things that both the young and the older should consider. Listen to your body and your mind, train your mind to come in sync with your body, and let them both become at one with your environment. As you explore the tributaries of your mind and body, do so with attentiveness, and without judgment or desire to take action. Learn to relax with inaction and be guided by your intuition to become one with every facet of your mind, body, spirit, and environment. This is the bliss that eludes many people who are unfortunately caught up with the daily routines of life. I oftentimes escape to the foothills of the North Jersey Palisades Mountains, along the Hudson River trails, and walk along the mountainous trails that skirt the river. During these mindfulness treks, I empty my mind of life's concerns and enjoy the bliss of the picturesque vegetation and the sounds of the river water beating against the shoreline rocks. Be attentive to your peace of mind!

A friend of mine who was terminally ill, and whose death was imminent, once told me that I should learn to listen to my body and pay keen attention to what my organs were communicating to me. The friend said that it is already too late when we see the doctor for a diagnosis. None of us is supposed to die prematurely from a curable condition. We should take a proactive approach in maintaining our physical and mental faculties. If you feel pain in your heart, do not wait until the following day to investigate the condition. Treat every message that your body sends you with urgency. A colleague of mine manifested symptoms of a stroke during the late evening hours. He indicated that his significant other pointed out to him that it appeared he was getting a stroke, but they went to bed without seeking medical assistance. My friend woke up in the morning with a massive stroke, which landed him in the hospital. He had to relearn to walk and talk. Fortunately for him, he recovered but not without some debilitating after-effects of the stroke. The outcome would have been significantly different if the matter was treated with urgency.

You need a healthy existence to enjoy the things that you achieved in life. You need a wholesome body, mind, and spirit to capitalize on the blessings that you have been afforded in this life. An old adage says that 'health is wealth'. You should first care for yourself before you consider caring for others. Do not compromise your health and happiness at the expense of the health and happiness of others. I have gone to doctors' offices, and it appeared as though they needed to check into the emergency room for an instant health examination. These doctors were there trying to preserve my life while their own lives were at stake. I am wondering whether you are in a similar predicament of trying to save everyone around you while you are in need of urgent attention. Your physical and mental health should be among the primary concerns, for both the young and the old.

Gone are the days when the quality of life was predicted primarily by chronological age. It is really true that the new 60 can be 40-looking and the new 70 can be 50-looking. Your health and longevity are not necessarily determined by your age. It is determined, for the most part, by how well you maintain yourself throughout your lifespan. I do understand that the family's health history can play a role in your longevity, but you have the ability to effectively manipulate your biological age by making healthy lifestyle choices. Change your mindset and convince yourself to live your best life now. Do not just say it but take the necessary steps to enhance your quality of life. Your longevity depends on it. There is nothing immoral about you wanting to live your best life now; a healthy and happy life grounded in positivity and meaningful undertakings. Positive energy is medicine for the mind, body, and spirit. Surround yourself with people who contribute to your happiness and those who challenge you to live your best life now. It is quite in order to live your remaining days filled with exhilaration and the realization of new frontiers. Make it your point of duty to be mindful of yourself.

Inevitabilities

Inevitability is something that is impossible to evade. Life has much inevitability. One of the first inevitabilities of life is that you are going to die sooner or later. One of these days, you are no longer going to be around to enjoy the wonderful things that life has to offer you at this moment. The day you are born, you involuntarily signed a contract with death; however, it is not prudent to preoccupy your mind with death and dying. It is best to preoccupy your mind with things pertaining to life. This mindset does not negate the fact that you have an expiration date. If you are a person of faith and believe in life after death, then you still should not be anxious about death and the end of human civilization. Focus on life and living. Focus on living your best life now. The nuances of life are unavoidable. You should not burden your mind with problems, conflicts, disappointments, hurts, pain, and sorrows. All of these annoyances will knock on your door while you are in the land of the living. There are no exemptions. You are not alone in dealing with unpleasant incidents in your life.

Some people are afraid to enjoy a happy moment because they believe that if they celebrate too much today, something bad will happen tomorrow. I have heard this self-defeating expression over and over again. Some people said that they would not talk about the wonderful things that are happening in their lives because the more they talk about them, the greater the chances are that bad things will follow. So, they live in this perpetual state of fear and avoid celebrating the good things that happen in their lives. This constant state of wondering what bad news is pending will rob one of the opportunities to fully embrace and enjoy the moment. Do not spend the limited number of hours given to you each day worrying about the future. Do not worry about tomorrow because tomorrow is not guaranteed. Whenever you have a happy moment, enjoy it to its fullest. Whenever something good happens in your life, celebrate it with uncensored enthusiasm. Live in the present. Deal with your challenges in real-time. Face your problems only when you are actually faced with them. Refrain from overthinking because it interferes with your potentialities.

I will have a degree of concern, but I will not be overly concerned about the future and what it may bring to the table. I am going to plan now for my imminent retirement, but I will not save all of my earnings in anticipation of emergency expenses and retirement. I know of people who worked very hard and saved the bulk of their earnings for retirement, only to develop health issues or face death at the point of retirement, or shortly thereafter. I have seen it happened to individuals with whom I was acquainted. You have to stop hoarding the bulk of your financial resources and enjoy some of it now. There is really no tomorrow. Today is the tomorrow that you spoke of yesterday. Live in the present!

Focus on your welfare and be generous to yourself. There is no point in driving a dilapidated vehicle if you have the financial resources to purchase a more comfortable and efficient one. If you are planning on updating the model of your vehicle, and it costs you a little more money than you had anticipated, go right ahead and close the deal. There is nothing that you are going to take with you to that grave. I have been to more funerals than I cared to go. On every occasion, with the exception of cremations, the ones who passed on were buried in one outfit. In certain cases, accessories such as jewelry were added. Some of the caskets were beautiful, and others were not particularly appealing to the eyes. If you should expire, please note that it is likely that all your assets would be divided among your beneficiaries, including some you probably did not care for during your lifetime. You pass this way but once, so you should be generous to yourself. Do something extraordinary for yourself today!

Self-indulgences

I frequently go to the park for cardiovascular exercises. Many times, while walking in the park, there are very few other individuals capitalizing on the facility. I often wonder why more people do not make full use of this free resource that is readily available. I realize that some people do not make it an intentional practice to take time and smell the roses. Too often, people spend quality time agitating themselves over situations that they cannot change rather than spending quality time nurturing their body, mind, and spirit. I hope to live to a good old age like my maternal grandmother, who died at 96. If I live to a good old age, I desire to approach my senior years with physical vitality, mental agility, social engagement, and spiritual reinvigoration. In your quest to live a healthy and fulfilled life, you may face criticism from those who do not share the value of taking quality time for maintenance of body, mind, and spirit. I can assure you that you will not be criticized by someone who has a good handle on taking care of their own existence and those who are making an effort to live a balanced life. Ignore the naysayers and continue taking care of yourself.

It is appropriate for you to take good care of yourself. It is commendable that you allot time to exercise. It is reasonable for you to be trendy. It is desirable for you to pamper yourself. Do not wait on others to indulge you because that may never happen. There is a thin line between being spiritual and being self-righteous. I do not know why some people who embrace religion are of the notion that, in order for people to be construed as being spiritual, they have to deny themselves of the finer things of life; the things that are geared towards making them live a balanced and fulfilled life right here on earth. Live your life without the intention of pleasing people and alignment with their self-serving expectations of you. Your amicable existence will likely conflict with the subjective ideals of the populace.

I live in Northern New Jersey, twelve miles from New York City, and for years a friend of mine could not get me to join him in the City, for an evening of relaxation. New York City is the mecca for diverse cultural expression and entertainment. I eventually decided to honor my friend's invitation. I remember boarding the bus at the designated bus stop, less than a block from my house, and proceeded on my journey to the Port Authority Bus Terminal in New York City. When I exited the bus in the City, my friend had to provide me with telephone navigation services from the point where I disembarked the bus to the ground floor of the Port Authority. It was a daunting task for me but I immensely enjoyed that evening in the City. That was the beginning of my frequent socializations in New York City. I have since discovered the gamut of social offerings that exist there. Stepping out of your comfort zone can lead you to situations that cater to your unmet needs and undiscovered delights.

I now travel to New York City on my own to capitalize on the wide array of amazing social events. For many years I was deprived of the rich cultural mecca that existed in New York City, a location that is less than half an hour commute from my New Jersey residence on a good traffic day. I now go there to listen to an entertaining jazz band, or to watch an engaging play. I also enjoy the benefit of being entertained by amazingly creative individuals who sing, act, draw, and dance on their own stages that they create on the sidewalks of Time Square. Prior to this exposure, I would be at home in my living room or in my man cave watching the news or a movie. Now I can hardly wait for an opportunity to indulge in the cultural mecca of New York City. These opportunities expand my options of the things available to me which are geared towards my happiness and peace of mind.

You cannot live an extraordinary life attending to everyone who knocks on your door or by spending your valuable time on social media. Get away from your safe place and indulge in the many rejuvenating activities that are accessible to you. Some of these activities are accessible to you at a minimal cost or at no cost at all. A dear friend of mine was afflicted with stomach cancer for four years before he succumbed to the ravages of the illness. For the last year of his life, he was fed through a tube. One day I visited him in the hospital, and he admonished me to eat well, now that I have the ability to eat. I recall his dear wife rubbing a piece of food on his lips, just so that his taste buds could relish the taste of food. Another terminally ill friend implored me to spend quality time enjoying my life, while I have health and strength. Some people are of the notion that there is a very thin line between wholesome enjoyment and immorality. That is not necessarily the case. This mindset is misleading and has caused many people to deprive themselves of wholesome entertainment, which could have rescued them from their mundane and frustrating lifestyles. A life lived under duress, anxiety, and sadness is undesirable and should be promptly transformed into one of bliss. Life is short so act now!

Occupy Until He Comes

For those who believe in the return of the Messiah, the tenets of your faith indicate that the event could occur at any time. It could occur today or at some point in the future. In the interim, you should live your best life now and purposefully work towards fulfilling your earthly destiny. Many years ago, when I was about to enroll in high school, my aunt told me that Jehovah would likely return to earth to establish his earthly kingdom, before it was time for me to graduate from high school. I graduated high school over four decades ago and subsequently completed many years of studies at the tertiary level. I got married, and I now have two adult children. Jehovah has not yet returned to establish his earthly kingdom and my aunt died several decades ago. Do not live your life obsessing over dying, death, and the afterlife. Keep your hope alive and simultaneously embrace the mandate, that there is some harmonious living, that you can enjoy right here on earth.

Every time there is a natural disaster or any other major catastrophe, some people of the Christian faith become hysterical, asserting that it is a sign of God's imminent return to earth. I spent most of my life in the 20th century, and my faith community during that era was told that, by the year 2000, God's second coming to earth would occur. At the writing of this manuscript, we are over two decades into the 21st century. Let me implore the people who are of the religious persuasion that, there is an imminent return of the Messiah, prepare yourselves spiritually as though the world will end today or tomorrow, but plan and embrace a fulfilled lifestyle in the interim. Your death might very well precede the realization of your hope in God's return. Some people will live to a good old age, while others will die prematurely at a relatively young age. I have an uncle who is currently in his mid-80s, and he could outwalk many people who are 30 years his junior. I officiated the funeral of a wonderful lady who died at the age of 99. In her late 80s, I witness this lady walked over 2 miles in the park. During her lifetime, this almost-centenarian was a fun-loving person. She loved people, and she exuded happiness. She did not sit down and wait for her life to be over. She occupied her place on earth and lived a fulfilled life until the time of her departure. I have witnessed several individuals who died at a much younger age. You do not know how long you are going to be alive, so live your best life now.

Get Over People

Let me reiterate. Do not spend your time preoccupying yourself with other people's solicitations and their dysfunctionalities. If you allow people to impose on you, they will be unrelenting in doing so. You give people permission to treat you the way you want to be treated. You must be aware that no matter how well you try to live your life, someone will judge you negatively. You have to get over people and get to the point where you care less about their impressions of you. Get over wanting to please the masses because that is an unattainable goal. If you think that you can live your life in such a way, that you have everybody approving of you, then you are destined to fail. Some people, who trade warm smiles with you and verbally affirm you, will discredit you with the same fervor in your absence. Please understand this harsh reality. So, do not live your life with the intent to be embraced by everybody. Embrace yourself. Live your life to please your maker and yourself, and be good towards humanity. Do not dwell on the positive reviews that people give to you because those reviews could be replaced by negative ones at any time. Do not give credence to the negative perceptions and bad reviews that uncaring people establish concerning you. Get over people!

The more you attempt to please people, the less regard some will have for you. The more you try to please people is the less value some will place on you. Assert yourself, exude positive energy, and go about your business exuberantly. Focus on your own life and your own affairs and refrain from getting into the habit of saving people from the consequences of their irresponsible choices. Some people may not care for you, yet they will publicly demonstrate respect towards you. Others may blatantly display disrespect towards you. Whatever the circumstance, never entertain or internalize any unsavory sentiments that others direct towards you. You may not be loved by some people but never allow yourself to be violated by their negative energy. Be most concerned about how you view yourself and how you align yourself with your values. If people are given the opportunity to distort your values and disrupt your journey to accommodate their own agenda, they will do so. Be watchful of these impositions and never allow anyone to cross the line with you. If you are impressionable and gullible, you will tend to position yourself to be used and manipulated by irrational people. In order to grow and excel, you must become unconcerned about impressing people, and base your rationalizations and decisions on your own premonitions and aspirations. Get people out of your business. Get over people.

Most relationships are transactional, and if you do not meet the stipulations of those attempting to fit you in their contract, you will no longer be of value to them. This has been a rude awakening for me, and I am sure it is for others. I have had some unfortunate occurrences in my life, and some of the people I thought would lend their support were visibly missing in action. There were individuals, who I considered close associates, and in whose lives I had sewn good deeds, but they never showed up to lend their support when I needed it. I learned the hard way that, some people engaged you because of the benefits that they could derive from the transaction. Be prepared to stand alone in your adversities and be thankful for those who support you unconditionally, during your troublesome times. You may be surprised to know that the people who neglected you during your tumultuous times are the first to congratulate you when you eventually prevail. Not everyone who celebrates with you in your season of success will be there for you during your season of trials. Get used to it and give precedence to yourself.

As much as I said that you should focus on your personal affairs and take good care of yourself, it is important you avail yourself to lend support to the less fortunate. Be sure that your motive for being there is selfless. Some people would never extend a helping hand to someone who is unable to return the favor. Seek to be there for those who truly need your support, even if they are unable to return the favor. Focus less on those who can already help themselves and are able to recompense you for your good deeds. Do not make it a practice to give of your resources to people who are not in need because your gesture may not be appreciated or valued. A small financial gift could make a significant difference in a needy person's life. A few words of encouragement to a lonely person could make a significant difference in that person's life. Engaging a person verbally and saying a few encouraging words, could significantly change a life for the better. Focus on what really counts.

Your legacy is determined not by how much you accumulate but by how much you positively impact those around you. If you want to continue living long after you are gone, then focus on the needy and be good to those who value your generosity. If you positively impact someone's life, then your living is not in vain. Show up for people when they need you the most. Be helpful towards others, but as you do so, make sure that it is not done at the expense of your own stability, security, and health. Avoid ungrateful people and those who display an attitude of entitlement. I implore you to stay focused on yourself and live your best life now.

Points to Ponder

   a. Take an inventory of your activities and the people with whom you associate

      i. Identify the people and things you are giving your attention

      ii. Determine how much they are aligned with your values

      iii. Categorize them based on the most to least important to you

   b. Abbreviate

      i. Be willing to adjust your vision and realign your efforts and interests

      ii. Be willing to consolidate your efforts to keep on track with your goals

      iii. Be willing to postpone plans for future consideration

   c. Eradicate

      i. Shun people who are a liability to your wellness and agenda

      ii. Eliminate plans that no longer align with your agenda

      iii. Disassociate yourself from what no longer works for you

   d. Regulate

      i. Maximize the time spent on the things that are of interest to you

    ii. Maximize the energy utilized on things that are of interest to you

   iii. Maximize the resources dedicated to things that are of interest to you

e. Elevate

    i. Enhance your peace of mind by adopting and celebrating positive changes

    ii. Make time for relaxation and rejuvenation

   iii. Purposefully pamper yourself regularly

Work towards a better representation of yourself and simultaneously celebrate all that you currently embody. Do not suspend the celebration of yourself for a future that is not guaranteed.

Reflections

_____

_____

_____

_____

_____

_____

_____

_____

_____

_____

_____

_____

_____

_____

_____

_____

_____

Chapter 6

It's Your Life

Do Not Allow Anyone To Dictate How You Should Live Your Life

★ ★ ★

One of the most significant and empowering hallmarks you can attain in life is the point where other people's subjective perceptions and judgments no longer dictate or color your self-concept, dictate your aspirations, or infringe on your peace of mind. You should never be governed by the expectations of your environment. You should live in the realm of your authentic self. You should be intentional in your quest for objectivity, your advocacy for tolerance, your respect for individuality, your abhorrence of mediocrity, and your mission for self-actualization. This is the essence of your destiny.

Mind Your Business

Have you relinquished your power to personally choose your most desirable lifestyle? If that is the case, you should consider reclaiming that power, and redirecting the affairs of your life. Do not give up the power to chart your own course and do not compromise your ability to live your best life now. I have been around for many years now, so I can no longer be categorized as a youngster. To live your best life, it is necessary for you to maintain a good physical and consistent mental rejuvenation. This requires that you put in the work in terms of frequent physical activities, balanced nutrition, and a wholesome mental health maintenance. Give a lot of attention to these three areas, and you will be on track for an incredible lifestyle.

It is interesting to note that, frequently people have indicated that I looked significantly younger than my actual chronological age, and for that I am grateful. I have absolutely no apprehension in affirming that I am aging well because it is the result of my relentless effort and hard work in maintaining a healthy lifestyle. It did not happen with me sitting on the couch. The moment you attempt to improve your lifestyle, you will be judged by others, but you cannot allow yourself to be distracted from your desire to improve the quality of your life. You cannot afford to live your life based on the approval of others. Imposing people tend to predetermine how you should live your life, but you have to vehemently reject the notion to live your life in a manner, that is geared towards pleasing others. These detractors will eventually concede and come to terms with the fact that you have resolved to live your best life, with or without their approval.

I attended the funeral of a 44-year-old man. That is a very young age for anyone to die. The mourners said some very admirable things about him. I proceeded to the internment and witnessed as the undertakers lowered his coffin in the grave. That lowering of the coffin was symbolic of finality and a permanent exodus from this earth. As I left the cemetery, I wondered whether, prior to his death, he had spent any time reminiscing over his life and entertained any regrets about the way he led his life. I also wondered whether he had lived the quality life that he desired. I am not thinking in terms of a house on a hill or the acquisition of a dream car. I am referring to him getting to the point where he could balance his life and had the opportunity to do the things that lead to a meaningful and happy existence. Did he feel great about the way he lived his life? Was his life inundated by stress? Did he allow cantankerous people to disrupt his peace of mind? Did he allow his mental space to be invaded by toxic individuals? Was he diligent in taking care of his physical health? Was he consistent in honoring his medical appointments? Did he follow the doctor's orders? Did he neglect to pay attention to his health? Did he disregard any signs that were alerting him of the serious medical condition that would eventually take his life at a relatively young age? If this young man had done an assessment of his 44 years on earth, and completed a self-evaluation, I am wondering what would have been his conclusion. Did he mind his business?

Self-evaluation

If you conduct an evaluation of your life and follow up with an analysis and objective assessment, do you believe that the outcome would suggest that you were living an exemplary lifestyle? Could you say that you are happy with the way you are currently living your life? I am not thinking in terms of material acquisition, academic status, or career satisfaction. I am talking about living optimally. When I say living optimally, I am talking about sustaining a peace of mind, happiness, and self-satisfaction. It is not normal for you to wake up every day feeling down. It is not normal to wake up every day feeling sad. It is not normal for you to wake up every day feeling inundated by anxieties which are precipitated by matters such as unrealized goals, other people's problems, negative information, and matters that are none of your business. You cannot afford to allow your reality to be such that you are always reacting to dilemmas.

I remember many years ago, I had three vehicles, and they were all in a state of disrepair at the same time. I decided not to let it become a crisis, so I parked all three cars and drove a 15-seater van to which I had access. I drove that 15-seater van for a long time. I did not worry about my dysfunctional vehicles. I was at peace, knowing that I did not have to concern myself with the expense of repairing these vehicles, at least not for a while. Some persons would have probably become obsessed about having these vehicles repaired. They would probably become obsessed with finding an appropriate mechanic to do the repairs, followed by worrying about the cost to repair the vehicles. Do not worry about things over which you have no control or which do not require your immediate attention. Worry has never solved a single problem.

Perhaps you have reached a certain age and have not yet realized some of your dreams. It is important that you reevaluate, and if necessary, make adjustments to your reality. Your perception of reality is important. You shouldn't pretend that your reality is in line with your expectations in life when you know that it is actually not. If there is a gap between your reality and your expectations, and that gap is not properly filled, then disappointment will ensue. Face your circumstances and be honest when assessing your disposition. Do not pretend to be satisfied just to appease those around you. Call a spade a spade, pick up the broken pieces, and carry on with your life with a focus on yourself.

It is desirable to maintain a lifestyle sustained by peace on the inside. It is also desirable to lead a lifestyle of waking up and feeling satisfied and excited concerning your existence. Some people fake their happiness sporadically, while others do so consistently. If you live your life void of satisfaction, then it is guaranteed that you will have regrets. You should take heed whenever life's circumstances confront you and force you to take stock of your journey. I can imagine how regretful you would feel, if at the end of your active days, you reflected and realized that you had not really lived the quality life that you desired. You should take a quality-of-life inventory on a regular basis to determine whether you are genuinely satisfied with the integrity of your existence. No one gets a second chance at living your best life because you pass this way but once. You should unapologetically take matters in your hands and ensure that you are on a path that leads to perpetual peace, sustained happiness, and continuous contentment.

Regrets

If you entertain regrets, then you are ungrateful for the growth you have attained. Embrace the teachable moments you have garnered from your experiences over the years. Do not spend your mental energy focusing on things you wish you had done differently. Everything that happens to you in life occurs for a specific purpose and is geared towards an outcome that places you on a trajectory that leads towards your destiny. Everything that happened to you in life contributed to the marvelous person that you are today. Like everyone else, you have made some mistakes, but you should refuse to be stunted by them. You have made some blunders throughout your life, but that is an inevitable part of the human condition. The best of us have made some horrible mistakes, and for some of them we are still dealing with the consequences. You might have made some decisions in the past which led to your own detriment, but I am sure that those were illuminating moments that provided you with valuable insights and tools to forge ahead with heightened prudence.

The person who you are today is the sum total of all the lessons learned from your past experiences. Allow these experiences to propel you to the stage where nothing disappoints you to the degree where you become dejected and devalued. The human species possess the capacity to realize noble feats, yet we also have the capability to do the most disdainful and dishonorable things. The best of us can find ourselves doing discreditable things, and the worst of us can find ourselves doing honorable things. Some people exploit others to accomplish their goal and it appears as though there are no consequences. Rational people can find themselves in the predicament where they chose an option which results in an undesirable outcome. These are facts of life for which you should not exhaust your thinking capacity seeking logical explanations. Life has dimensions of complexity that will leave you with more questions than answers. Learn to deal with whatever is put on your plate. Function to the best of your ability and apply the lessons learned from your experiences. Your best is good enough.

You should understand and embrace the fact that both good and bad things will happen to you. That is a fact of life, and it should be accepted along with all the other facts of life. A part of living involves dealing with the vicissitudes that you face from day-to-day. A part of living also has to do with navigating the ups and the downs that you encounter from day-to-day. I was once driving in Manhattan, and indicated that I intended to make a right turn, not knowing that drivers were only allowed to make such a turn at designated times. A traffic enforcement officer observed when I was about to make the turn, and did not give an indication that it was an illegal turn. He patiently waited for me to make the illegal turn and then issued me a ticket for a traffic violation. Some of the things that occur to us, could have been avoided if others would only give us an indication, which we needed to make an adjustment to our undertaking. It is not a requirement but a moral obligation to provide meaningful feedback as we interface with those around us. Life is not always fair, so do not be bent out of shape when you are faced with situations that could have been avoided, if only others had acted empathetically. Discount your damages, and roll with the punches, then take a deep breath and carry on.

Come to the understanding that life is not over when you are constricted by the tentacles of discomforting intrusions. Do not allow disillusionment to cripple you. When challenged with the payment of a delinquent bill, be sure to communicate with your creditors and negotiate a manageable payment plan. Be as pleasant as you possibly can, even if the creditor is obnoxious. Always negotiate a reasonable reduction in the outstanding bill. You could possibly end up paying only a fraction of the original bill. If you are unable to honor the negotiated agreement, do not neglect the matter. Call back and renegotiate another payment agreement. You should not ignore a problem indefinitely because that will not cause it to disappear. Do not resort to avoidance but be solutions-oriented in all matters. You should always seek to relieve yourself of pressure and stressful situations. If you have a stressful job that you cannot afford to leave at the moment, then adjust your attitude and do the best you can. It is inevitable that you will be faced with a certain degree of stress, while engaging in a certain assignment. Focus on the task at hand, work around the stressful condition, tackle the assignment, and unwind the best way you can at the end of the work day. Go for a walk in the park or engage in some other activity to relieve you of your stress. Make it a habit to untangle yourself of all distractions before you retire for bed each night. Protect your quality of rest.

Don't Worry

Enjoy yourself. Dedicate quality time for yourself. If you realize that you are about to be inundated by a stressful situation, get away physically and mentally from the situation and seek solace in a nonintrusive environment. Connect with a pleasant person. Find a pleasant place to go. Take a stroll along the scenic locale and enjoy the calming effects of nature. This will get your mind settled and allows you to develop a rational approach in responding to the situation. You cannot afford to live a bothersome life because the ultimate price for doing so is very high.

Some years ago, I had a health scare, and I had to do several medical examinations and invasive tests. Most of the tests were done in a cancer center facility. Every time I visited the center, I was in the company of some very visibly sick and mostly elderly people. The walls of the reception area were decked with information about terminal illnesses. The television monitors suspended on the walls displayed vivid messages concerning terminal diseases and their associated symptoms. During these visits, I mostly travelled alone, and honestly, I was not casually fearful, but I was intensely scared. I tried to figure out a way of reducing my fear factor, but that task was unattainable. When it was time for me to do the last and most serious test, my son and a dear friend accompanied me to the urologist. I acted composed and fearless; however, both my son and my friend later indicated to me that my mannerisms clearly displayed extreme nervousness.

I completed my gamut of tests and received a clean bill of health from the urologist. When I reflected on the situation, I realized that my worry was in vain. I was subjected to all the abuse that takes place in the human body as a result of my anxiety. If I had remained composed all along, I would have saved myself from many weeks of worry with its debilitating effects. Worry is an imposing negative emotion which can be regulated and even abated. Unfortunately for me, I accommodated the fear factor throughout testing procedures and my peace of mind was disrupted throughout the entire process. Interestingly, I was least anxious during my culminating visit. I attribute this degree of composure to the support that I received from my son and my dear friend who accompanied me. There will be times when it becomes difficult for you to travel a leg of your journey alone. It is advisable that you surround yourself with a few caring friends who will lend you a shoulder to lean on, especially during the times when you need it most. It is vital that you find a way to move forward in the face of adversity.

Make the decision to stop worrying about life. Stop worrying because your worry cannot change anything for the better. Take control of your journey and celebrate each step with all that it brings. Stop being regretful about missed opportunities, unaccomplished goals, and unrealized expectations. There will be people who are more accomplished than you in certain aspects of life. There will be people who reside in a more luxurious home in a safer environment than yours. There will be people who drive a more prestigious car than yours. There may be individuals who you consider more attractive than yourself. Depending on who is doing the observation, the assessment about you may range anywhere along the continuum from good to ghastly. You have the prerogative to evaluate and either reject or accept the assessment others have of you. You should be tentative in subscribing to the assessment of others, whether good or bad, because these judgments can be subjective, transient and changeable. Conduct your own self-assessment, celebrate the positive things about yourself and make improvements where necessary. Establish your own rubric for the governing of your life.

You may not be financially endowed, but money does not provide all the solutions to life's problems. If that were the case, there would not be so many unhappy rich people. Many rich people and many poor people are unhappy alike. Some resort to drugs and other unhealthy choices in an effort to forge a peace of mind. Both rich and poor people occasionally resort to suicide in an attempt to stop their pain. Do not allow life's dejections and pitfalls to cause you to make irrational decisions. Nothing deprives you of your energy and motivation than living in a stressful space. Embrace whatever comes your way with grace, patience, and optimism. Accept life for what it is, not in terms of resigning yourself to your adverse situations, but by confronting the impediments that face you and finding courage to cultivate an action oriented mindset. This approach will empower you with an attitude of hopefulness. If the need arises, modify your goals to make them more attainable. Identify resources to help you advance towards your goals. Once there is a desire to move ahead, then there is the possibility of negotiating a solution.

Rerouting

It is a reality of life that, with the passage of time, certain desires may not be realized in your life. Understand that you sometimes have to make adjustments to your goals, based on the direction that your journey takes you. Life does not always evolve in the manner we expected. We all will experience disappointments along the journey. You might be trying to figure out why random things occur to you even though you have been proactive in your approach. You may find yourself facing predicaments that you never remotely anticipated. Things will happen to you that require a change of direction. Sometimes you will have to make adjustments to your original plans, and at other times you may have to make new plans. The alternative to this is that you will settle for an undesirable option. Take control of the present, and the future will align itself with whatever adjustments you have to make along the way. Stay on your own path because only your designated path will lead you to your pre-ordained destiny. I studied the sciences in high school and at the undergraduate level; however, for most of my professional life, I have served as a public school administrator focusing on student support services. You should not be so inflexible and set in your ways that you become unresponsive to the possibility of change.

There are those of you who are really unhappy. Deep down on the inside, you are unfulfilled. You might be married, or you might be single, but you are unhappy. You might be poor or rich, but you are unhappy. You may have an appealing physical structure, but you are unhappy. You may have a great job or a great career, but you are unhappy. You might be young, middle-aged or older, but you are unhappy. You may have periods of happiness, but generally, you are unhappy. You get up each day and carry out your customary activities, but at the end of the day, you retreat to your place of dissatisfaction. If any aspect of this description resonates with you, then it is time to do a reality check and take the first steps towards enhancing your lifestyle.

Nurture good friendships and do not be averse to entertain new friendships. Embrace friends who will support you in circumventing the challenges of life. I have intentionally and consistently taken steps to improve all aspects of my quality of life. I have particularly taken steps to invigorate my social life. I was socially awkward for a long time because my waking hours were spent primarily focusing on everybody else's welfare and neglecting my own. One day, I was awaked to the realization that I was missing out on so many wonderful and wholesome indulgences that life had to offer. I identified individuals who could assist me in enhancing the neglected social dimension of my life. If you are not as socially engaging as you desire, talk to people who have been intentional in living a fulfilled social life and solicit their assistance in guiding you towards a socially enriched lifestyle.

Be sure that you connect with individuals who are more open-minded and spontaneous than you are. If you are happy only in appearance, then you owe it to yourself to get the assistance you need to ensure your genuine happiness. Balance your life. Take care of the physical dimension of your life. Take care of the mental dimension of your life. Take care of the social dimension of your life. Take care of the spiritual dimension of your life. If you take care of these four dimensions of life, then be assured that you will evolve into an incredibly fulfilled person. I intend to leave this life as a balanced and fulfilled human being. I intend to go out with a smile on my face, thanking my creator for giving me the wisdom to live an amazingly fulfilled life. It is never too late to start. It does not matter how you have lived in the past; the important thing is that you take charge of your journey today and live your best life now, and for the duration of your remaining days on earth.

Now

I thought about life and realized that irrespective of your age, all the guaranteed time you have at your disposal is the current moment. Tomorrow you may never rise to face the sunshine or rain, so live your best life now. No one is guaranteed tomorrow. The teenager has no advantage over the senior citizen when it comes on to living in the moment. Today is the tomorrow that we spoke about yesterday. Technically there is no tomorrow. All you have is today, so live your best life now. I guess that by now you know why some very elderly people wake up every day with a smile on their faces and a plan to execute. I am convinced that the wise and elderly people have learned that the present moment is the only guaranteed time that we all have at our disposal. Armed with this knowledge, one needs to cherish every living moment in time. When your life on earth approaches the inevitable end, your plan should be to live your last days and moments with no regrets. Your desire should be to smile all the way to the other side with an assurance that you have spent your days living your best life. It's never too late to start living your best life. Start your journey towards living your best life today!

I have celebrated many significant milestones in my life. I have accomplished most of the major goals that I established for myself. These goals include spiritual enrichment, raising two amazing children alongside my wife Carmen, acquiring a comfortable house, purchasing my dream car, earning a terminal degree, and enjoying a fulfilling career. Accomplishing these goals did not translate into the degree of happiness that I thought I would have gained. In fact, after accomplishing these goals, I realized that the joy associated with these triumphs was not sustained. True happiness evaded me. For a while I settled for the good life, instead of the great life, and endured the dissatisfaction of an emotionally dysfunctional existence. Do not settle for a good life; it is the enemy of a great life. I subscribe to Jim Collins' principles on this. In his book entitled, *Good To Great,* he illustrated that good is the enemy of great. Whether you have 1, 10, 30, or 50 more years of life, it is your personal obligation to ensure that this time is spent living your best life. Commit yourself to living your best life starting right now!

Ensure that your remaining time on earth is your happiest and most fulfilled leg of your journey. Commit yourself to effectively managing all four dimensions of your very existence; the physical, mental, spiritual and social. If you take stock of your life, you just may discover that you are yet to live your best life. It is unfortunate that some people have found themselves under spheres of influence that either covertly or overtly dictate their quality of life. Some people are afraid to step out of their comfort zone or from under the influence of a social system to pursue a better lifestyle. They do this for acceptance into a community or for fear of being judged by others. You should become unrelenting in your pursuit of happiness because the limited time you have to experience a better life is slipping away moment by moment. When you eventually embark on a path towards a fulfilled life, you will become more fully aware of the deprivations to which you have been subjecting yourself. Once you become liberated from the confines of a mundane lifestyle, you will become increasingly undisturbed by the manipulators and skeptics who once hijacked your freedom to live your best life now.

Fear Not

Never judge others based on their unique or unfamiliar paths. Neither should you entertain others who solicit you to join them in their skepticism of those who are brave enough to choose paths that lead to living their best life now. Do not be afraid to be judged for doing what is right for you. Your journey is your personal prerogative. If you live to appease people and you die without living your best life, the appeased will probably attend your funeral and may even shed a tear. They may even speak very well of you posthumously and echo how wonderful a person you had been. The sad reality is that you would have already been dead without experiencing the quality of life you desired. You are placed on the face of the earth to enjoy the journey as you fulfill your assignment. It is an incredible blessing to be able to take delight in the joys of your journey and relish in the fulfillment of sustained happiness and peace of mind.

You have a personal obligation to enjoy your life. I used to be a lover of music during my youthful years. During my early college years in my twenties, I would study while soft background jazz filled the atmosphere. As I grew older and assumed more responsibilities in life, I stopped listening to music without even realizing it. In recent years, as I became intentional in living my best life now, I rekindled my love for music with an even greater appreciation. It was only when I decided to reinvigorate my life, that I regained my appreciation for music. Music has once again become one of my favorite pastimes. It brings about that feeling of peace and tranquility. It causes me to lighten up. I also regained my love for dancing. I attended several ballroom dance events and it was electrifying, refreshing, and rejuvenating. Ballroom dancing was a new genre of dance for me but each year I negotiated my way around the dance floor without any significant collisions. Lighten up now and be daring enough to tackle new and interesting undertakings because you may have a very limited time to indulge yourself in the finer things of life.

I do not know the length of my days, but I can assure you that, for now, and for the rest of my active days I will be maintaining a wholesome existence. I will persistently aim to maintain my physical health. I will continue in my aspiration to maintain a healthy mental state. I will continue to be in pursuit of an authentic spiritual life. I also intend to capitalize on the wonderful and wholesome social offerings that spark my interest. I am working on these goals consistently and judiciously. Make a decision to work towards experiencing your best life now, and for the remainder of your days!

Points to Ponder

a. Establish ownership

    i.   Acknowledge the right to manage your life

    ii.   Own the responsibility to manage your life

    iii.   Assert the power to manage your life

b. Anticipate uncertainty

    i.   Become accepting of the fact that anything can change at any given time

    ii.   Be assured that you have alternative plans or options in case situations change

    iii.   Activate your creativity in case change becomes necessary

c. Do not be intimidated by rejection

    i.   Do not take it personally when what you represent is rebuffed

    ii.   Do not compromise your values or defend your worth

    iii.   Respond instead of reacting negativity

d. It's often better to ask forgiveness than for permission

    i.   Do not always wait for others to dictate your actions

    ii.   Take chances and make decisions in order to move the agenda forward

iii. If you are wrong, then ask for pardon; if you are right, then your decision sets the precedence

e. Do not be averse to change

i. Be willing to abandon anything that inhibits your progress

ii. Be willing to change the status quo and activate positive change

iii. Be willing to pursue new opportunities and untapped possibilities

A real friend walks with you and embraces your ideals and challenges when the rest of the world walks around you and awaits the outcome.

Reflections

Chapter 7

Get Your Mind Right
Build Up Your Mental Tenacity

★ ★ ★

It's your emotional response to the adversities of life that determines growth and maturity. Challenges are inevitable in the grand scheme of things, and it's the way you respond to them that shapes your identity. You are innately a champion, and therefore it is incumbent upon you to respond appropriately to the infringements that life imposes upon you.

Mind Care

Many daunting things will happen to you along life's journey. If you are able to understand what is happening and why it is happening, then half of the problem is already solved. I have seen so many individuals having to deal with insurmountable challenges. Many people succeeded in their quest to overcome their challenges because their minds were attuned to confronting and resolving them. The mental tenacity of these individuals has inspired me. The mind is a very powerful tool. It is like a two-edged sword. It can build you up, and it can tear you down. If you do not know how to regulate it, then the mind has the potential to inflict devastation on every aspect of your life. If you know how to regulate your mind, you will be more equipped to effectively deal with your adversities. The mind is also like a knife. You can use a knife in the preparation of a scrumptious meal in the kitchen, but the same knife can be used as a deadly weapon. If handled recklessly, even though its uses were intended for the right purpose, the knife could cause significant damages. With this in mind, you should handle your mind with care.

According to the National Institute of Mental Health Disorders, an estimated 26% of Americans, ages 18 and older, suffer from a diagnosable mental disorder in a given year. This represents about 1 in 4 adults. The same statistics showed that each year approximately 9.5% of American adults, ages 18 and over, will suffer from a depressive illness such as major depression, bipolar disorder, or dysthymia.

You can touch your eye. You can feel your heart. If your ear is aching, you can massage it. These, and other organs, are all tangible parts of your body that can be attended to with precision. If there is a physical dysfunction in the body, in most cases, it can be rectified with the appropriate medical assistance or with tender and loving care. People are inclined to pay more attention to their physical health than their mental health. If you are inflicted with a physical condition, then you would most likely consult with a physician in an effort to alleviate the problem. The mind is a very powerful component of human functioning. When faced with a mental condition, people tend not to approach it in the same manner or with the same degree of urgency as they would, if faced with a physical problem. More often than not, they expect the mental problem to correct itself without purposeful interventions. More often than not, and to the detriment of the persons with the mental dysfunctions, the mind does not always autocorrect. You need to pay attention to your mind, not just as it relates to its thinking capacity, but also in terms of determining whether there is an underlying mental disorder. Based on my interactions, I realize that many people suffer from what appears to be undiagnosed mental problems. Some individuals are able to function acceptably in their day-to-day lives even though they are experiencing significant mental health issues. There are many people who, once they get into the seclusion of their home and close the door, battle with mental dysfunctionalities. This is a battle that is fought in isolation by many people. Take care of your mind!

Mental Dysfunction

Some people fall asleep and wish not to be wakened in the morning to face another day, and others battle with suicidal thoughts. The high suicidal rate is attributed to the prevalence of mental illness. People will appear to be quite normal, and then you later learn that they took their own lives. You may think that this will never impact you or your loved ones, but no one is exempt from the possibility of suffering from mental challenges. You may be dealing with your own mental issues, and not realizing that you have a clinical problem requiring treatment. Pay attention to your mental health. Pay attention to your emotions. Pay attention to your feelings. If you do not feel mentally well, then do not keep it as a secret. You should seek professional intervention or talk to someone who is able to point you in the right direction for the appropriate mental health resources.

I received a call from an individual who felt overwhelmed. This person was crying profusely while attempting to describe to me what was happening. The person was unable to identify what triggered this intense emotional reaction. I spent some time listening attentively to the person's expressions and responded with clarifying questions. The person did not initially fully understand the intense emotional reaction. After an honest conversation, the person was able to identify the trigger that precipitated the intense emotional response, and this resulted in a breakthrough to recovery. It is sometimes difficult to gain insights into your own mental challenges without the intervention of someone equipped with the skillset to facilitate you in the recovery process.

The first thing some individuals resort to when faced with mental challenges is to conceal their problems from their friends and loved ones. They enter the privacy of their room, shut the windows, lock the doors, turn off the lights, and retreat into seclusion. They also turn off the phone and refrain from communicating with anyone. This is ultimately a self-destructive approach to take in these instances because it is very difficult for anyone to deal with mental issues without support. We are social beings who typically interact at some level with others; it is the natural thing to do. Mental issues, if left unattended, will drive you into an enclave of isolation. Please note that you are not as mentally resilient as you may think. You may assume that you have a tremendous mental fortitude, but it is not until you are faced with mental challenges that you will realize how ill-equipped you are in dealing with them on your own. Mental illnesses are often not easily predicted. If you find yourself in a mentally disruptive state, please seek counseling and therapy before the condition progressively gets worse.

Mental Illness Triggers

So why are mental health conditions so prevalent? Oftentimes mental problems are genetic. Your struggle with mental problems might be related to a parent or grandparent who struggled with a similar condition. Do not blame yourself and do not blame your family. You contributed nothing to this pre-existing condition, and neither did your implicated family members. You inherited the trait. You could also develop mental problems based on a traumatic experience that you have encountered. You did not ask for that traumatic experience, but it occurred to you. It was not self-imposed, so do not assume the blame. There are so many people who are dealing with mental health issues because of unresolved trauma. These unresolved concerns are not addressed because of various reasons, one of which is that the afflicted person may not be inclined to disrupt the status quo or hurt a significant other. You should not ignore the debilitating effects of your traumatic encounter. You cannot overcome your problem or alleviate your pain by ignoring it. You could repress the effect of your trauma for days, months and even years, but it will most definitely resurface at some point in time, and to your detriment.

Abuse is a common traumatic experience. You might have been the survivor of abuse. Maybe your parents were abusive toward you. Maybe your siblings were abusive. Maybe you are the victim of an abusive relationship. Maybe you were bullied by your peers. Some of the young people whose mental dysfunction resulted in them committing heinous crimes were victims of one type of abuse or another. They internalized the trauma, and no one was observant enough to recognize the unspoken cry for help. If you are faced with the trappings of a toxic environment, you could experience major trauma; the outcome of which may not be readily manifested, but the latent effects will present themselves at an inopportune time. Whatever the factor that compromises your mental health, it is important that you identify its impact and seek the necessary mental health care that is geared towards your recovery. It is very important that you prioritize your mental care. Your mental health is important. This cannot be overemphasized. You probably think that you are strong and capable enough to personally take care of your mental issues, but just as how it is unlikely for patients to conclusively diagnose and treat their physical illness, it is equally unlikely that you will be able to do the same for your mental illness.

I was involved in a very major accident that could have taken my life. The motor vehicle was totaled with a riddled engine and crushed frontal area. I escaped with an insignificant injury to my hand, but it left me mentally traumatized. It took me a while to overcome the trauma that this near-death experience imposed upon me. Fortunately for me, I had a good support system from which I gained sustained emotional support. My greatest challenge during that process was the incessant refocusing of my mind in an effort to curb the frequency and intensity of the disturbing related flashbacks. My swift and compelling recovery is attributable to the support I received during this period of mental turmoil. If you think about your traumatic experience too hard, too long, and too frequently, it will surely overwhelm and consume you. It is important that you have an appreciation for, and an understanding of, the causative factors for mental instability. It is also important that you have insights into the various interventions that can be employed in addressing mental challenges. It is advisable and appropriate for you to consult with a mental health specialist for assistance in dealing with your mental concerns. Professional counseling has proven to be an effective response in averting or controlling mental health problems. Professional counseling helps in understanding, evaluating and navigating the arduous and sometimes painful path to recovery and sustained wholesomeness.

Mental health professionals are equipped to assist you in coming to terms with the mind's unresolved matters. These professionals are specifically trained to assist you. They are able to identify what is happening to you and effectively assist with the recovery process. I was asked to facilitate a crisis counseling session with a grieving group of people because a young man from that social circle had lost his life under tragic circumstances. During my session, I focused on the understanding of post-traumatic stress disorder and effective ways in dealing with trauma. Following my presentation, I realized that sitting in the audience were many people experiencing unrelated, equally intense, traumatic afflictions. Many of them approached me following the presentation and shared the trauma with which they had been contending, some of them for many years. Some individuals indicated to me that they did not realize their symptoms were directly related to past traumatic experiences. In order to live your best life now you have got to get your mind right!

The Power Of Knowledge

Knowledge is power. Educate yourself concerning your mental health and the mental health condition of your loved ones. It could save you heartache and pain. If a mental health professional apprises you of a prevailing mental condition, then address it immediately. Do not resort to denial or self-pity. It is not the end of the world. Educate yourself about the condition. You have access to innumerable resources for mental health concerns. Participate in workshops and support groups that focus on mental health. Become intentional in learning all you can about mental health and its collateral effects. So, become as knowledgeable as you possibly can on the subject. Once you visit a mental health provider and identify your condition, you should take the next steps towards ensuring your recovery. If you are not feeling mentally rejuvenated, if you are suffering from insomnia, if you are frequently depressed, then view these symptoms as telling signs that you are in need of a mental evaluation. Having a mental condition does not mean that you are insane. Securing mental health care from a psychiatrist, psychologist, or professional counselor is nothing for which to be ashamed. You would probably be surprised if you become aware of the myriads of people, with whom you are associated, who are receiving mental health treatment. There are many people with mental challenges, who receive the appropriate treatment and are living bountifully. If you are suffering from a mental health condition, get the professional help you need to ascertain your recovery.

The adversities that I have contended with throughout my life have ultimately enhanced my mental fortitude. For many years I focused on everything and everyone other than myself. At various periods in my life I faced significant personal challenges that weighed on my mental resources. In order to address this predicament, I sedated myself with work, setting and achieving major academic, personal and professional goals. Additionally, I focused on every other task that was in the scope of my abilities. This was done in an attempt to take my focus off my personal challenges. My job reviews and evaluations were outstanding, and my resume was impressive, but my mental and physical health was on the decline. I was not sleeping well at nights, and I was fatigued during the days. I was always on edge. I was impatient and easily upset. My mood swings were frequent and unpredictable. I knew that something was radically wrong, but I was unable to identify the cause. I recognized that I needed help, and I reached out for it.

I eventually went to my primary care physician for a physical evaluation. My doctor informed me that I was not in the best of health but with proper nutrition and exercise I could bring my health back on track to full recovery. My nutritionist told me that my health could be severely compromised if I did not immediately change my lifestyle. I heeded the warning and changed my lifestyle. As I changed my lifestyle, both my physical and mental health improved dramatically. I started going to the gym consistently, and I hired a personal trainer. I changed my nutrition and started eating healthier. I retired to bed earlier at night, and I was no longer battling insomnia. I stopped remaining in the office at work for prolonged periods after my workday ended; consequently, I enjoyed more relaxation time at home and at the park. I learned how to assertively decline additional responsibilities at work. Instead of hoarding and rolling them over, from year to year, I utilized more of my vacation days to engage in relaxing and enjoyable activities. I learned how to stop and smell the roses. I lost about thirty pounds. My mind was rejuvenated. I slept like a baby at nights. I had a much more amicable personality. I felt better emotionally and looked much better physically. Friends and associates asked about the secret for the major positive changes that they observed in my demeanor. My significant others articulated their preference for this new version of me. The secret was that I prioritized my personal affairs and learned how to balance my life and focus on me. I changed my life for the better! Take time to focus on yourself!

Bad Things Happen To Good People

If you are striving to do your best, and yet faced with challenging impositions that are causing insurmountable strain on your mental faculties, do not be dismayed. This is not a unique phenomenon. Please note that bad things do happen to good-intentioned people. Be consoled in knowing that you are not alone in dealing with this perplexing wonderment. There are countless good human beings who are strapped with recurring misfortunes. Be assured that some of the mishaps that you face are not as extreme as the ones that other good human beings have to face. The positive thing about this is, you are still here in the land of the living and you have the ability to fully recover and tell your story. So, rise up and take the necessary steps towards your healing. Cultivate and apply the resilience that is required to confront and overcome your mind-blowing tribulations. Take matters into your own hands and change your position!

Some people with tremendous potential remain in an unhealthy mental state and become victims of their circumstances. They are perplexed over the fact that even though they did the best they could in life, misfortunes constantly knocked on their doors. Your misfortune may be in the form of a toxic relationship, an unexpected divorce, loss of job, or an unforeseen financial challenge; among other possible challenges. You might not have anticipated these horrible things happening to you. Whatever the circumstance, you should not just sit back and assume the victim stance of inaction, but arise and build up your mental tenacity. You might not be able to do it on your own, but take matters into your hands and embrace credible strategies that are geared towards restoration of your wholesomeness.

Life's challenges do not discriminate. Everyone is susceptible to some type of derailment. Life happens. Sometimes you might not even be able to pinpoint the things that disrupt your carefully planned goals and aspirations. Instead of trying to figure it out on your own, engage an expert who will effectively guide you along the road to recovery and reset. Life can be beautiful. You do not have to live in a mansion on a hill for life to be beautiful. You do not have to be driving a Lamborghini for life to be beautiful. When you build up your mental tenacity, there is no obstacle that you will not be able to conquer and there is no obstruction that can come your way that you cannot tackle and dominate. There is no danger that can come in your path that you cannot overcome.

Activate your will to be an overcomer and rid yourself of self-destructive tendencies and thoughts. Your mental dysfunctions can become so familiar that you accept them as a normal part of your existence. Reject that notion! Do not resign yourself to the entrapments of your hindrances. They are temporary. No one should be going to bed at nights and constantly struggling to fall asleep. Everyone deserves the gratification of a good night's rest. The quality of your night's rest will determine the quality of the following day. When your abnormality becomes your normalcy, then the unfolding path of your destiny will become distorted. Adversities are inevitable for us all. Challenges in life are inevitable. Mental health care is of paramount importance. Protect your mental space. Whatever you have to change to secure your mental sanity, be unrelenting in doing so. Be undeterred in your quest to facilitate positive changes in your life. As you pursue the path to change, constantly remind yourself that the bad things that happen to you are not a judgment on your character but a new tool in your arsenal to deal with whatever obstacle that faces you in the future. Every test you face is designed to thrust you towards your destiny. There is a purpose for every struggle that you encounter. Turn your misfortunes into growth opportunities!

Mind Management

The health of your mind is very important. If you have a weak mental constitution, then other aspects of your functioning will likely be affected in some manner. It is expected that at times the state of your mental health will be compromised, but this should be the exception and not the norm. When you have a strong mental constitution, you will be better able to contend with the things that weigh on your emotions. Your emotions were not designed to lead you. You were designed to manage your emotions. Your mind was designed to regulate your emotions. If your emotions dictate your responses, then you are destined for despondency. If given the reigns, your untamed emotions will cause you to make permanent decisions in your quest to address temporary problems. You do not want to find yourself in such a predicament because sometimes the consequences for irrational decisions are devastating and irreversible. So, it is required of you to discipline your mind in managing your emotions. You can effectively manage your emotions when your mind is fortified.

Some people strive to ascend the social ladder with an expectation that the higher they climb, the less likely they will encounter mental woes. To the contrary, it appears as though the higher you advance up the social ladder, the more challenges you are prone to face. This is partially so because there is a tendency for your social circle to shrink as you climb the social ladder. Throughout my life, I set short-term and long-term goals, and I usually accomplish them. At a particular juncture in my life, as I was realizing some major professional and personal goals, I was faced with unsurmountable problems which targeted me from unique and unexpected angles. My mental stability was challenged, and I needed to take action to maintain my sanity. I would wake up very early in the mornings and jog in the park before I headed out to work. I would sometimes jog late in the evenings. I would engage in strength training on a regular basis. I became an active member of the gym. I improved my nutrition. I drank a lot of water. These actions, among others, fortified my mind and kept me focused on the things that really mattered. Sometimes people seek after spectacular methodologies to resolve their problems when they have free, effective, and accessible resources at their disposal. Mother Nature provides a plethora of resources that can help in the process of healing the mind, body and spirit.

In order to maintain a healthy frame of mind, you must be at peace with yourself. Learn to be comfortable with yourself and learn to enjoy your own company. Social interaction is important, but you do not necessarily need people around you continuously to be happy. You do not always need people in your physical and mental space to be happy. Your happiness is a personal choice. In certain instances you can make peace with your past predicaments, but it is impossible to change any of your past encounters. Your past is history. Do not allow yourself to be anchored to the past. Start living your best life today without the stigmas of yesterday. The way you lead your life going forward is what really counts towards your happiness and fulfillment. How are you planning on living your life as of today? Start with making a commitment to live a better life effective immediately. Relinquish your focus on others and start focusing on yourself now. You should evolve to a zone of comfort where you intentionally focus on what counts most; and, above all else, you certainly count most. The time to take the steps for the enhancement of your quality of life is now. The sacrifices you need to make in order to effectively manage your mental health should be done promptly and without hesitation. Get your mind right!

Points to Ponder

a. Come to terms with the vulnerabilities of your mind

    i. Accept the fact that you are not mentally invincible

    ii. Pay attention to the factors that can potentially destabilize the mind

    iii. Respond to your mental ailments as you would to your physical ailments

b. Be sensitive to the threats that intrude on your mental space

    i. Become aware of the onset of your mentally unsettling triggers

    ii. Take note of what causes your mentally unsettling triggers

    iii. Become attuned to your responses and to your mentally unsettling triggers

c. Confront situations that attack your mental health

    i. Identify the source of your mental disturbance

    ii. Face the source of your mental disturbance

    iii. Eradicate or subjugate the source of your mental disturbance

d. Seek help for the maintenance of your mental health

    i. Research credible mental health resources

    ii.   Identify the appropriate resources to address your mental health concerns

    iii.   Select and utilize the mental health services that best meet your need

  e. Guard your mental space

    i.   Disassociate from people who are a threat to your mental health

    ii.   Disengage from activities that are a threat to your mental health

    iii.   Desist from indulging with any entity that threatens your mental health

Guard yourself against mental manipulators. In their attempt to avoid feeling guilty about the inappropriate things they impose upon you, unscrupulous persons will deliberately and presumptuously pretend they are innocent and broadcast that you are the culpable party. They create chaos and conflict as a distraction to soothe or justify their unscrupulous and narcissistic behaviors. Do not seek to justify yourself because truth needs no defense. Be confident and comforted in the assurance of your innocence. Ignore the perpetrators and safeguard your sanity.

Reflections

Chapter 8

Swim Against The Current

Advance Yourself By Any Necessary And Credible Means

★ ★ ★

The complexities of life, coupled with the nuances of inner conflicts, and self-imposed limitations, are sometimes overwhelming. These vicissitudes, though daunting, should be seen as steppingstones and building blocks to enhance your capacity for personal growth and resilience. They can fuel your engine and ignite a flaming fire of potentiality within the scope of your reality.

Roll With The Punches

Sometimes life takes a turn for the better, and sometimes it takes a turn for the worse. Sometimes you get pleasant surprises, and sometimes you get unpleasant surprises. It is of paramount importance that you have a mindset to put one foot in front of the other and move forward every day. Life has so many more ups and downs than we ever anticipated. For those who have never really faced adverse situations, you might not be able to relate to the unsurmountable hardships that some people encounter over their lifetime.

I was called at three o'clock in the morning by one of my close friends. She asked that I come to her home immediately. When I got there, she told me that her husband had suddenly passed and that his body was lying in the basement family room. I was never before faced with a tragic circumstance of this nature. I joined her in the basement, along with her best friend and another associate. Her husband lay there, motionless. He did not appear to be dead. He appeared to be in a deep sleep. My friend told me that her husband never returned to their bedroom within a reasonable time and so she checked the basement family room to see whether he was fine. She found the lifeless body of her husband in his special chair. We all sat there and grappled with what to say. No one seemed to find the appropriate words to say, and so we sat in silence, for the most part, waiting for the undertaker to come and take the body to the morgue. How does one react to such tragic circumstances? Throughout this ordeal, my friend remained composed while, oblivious to her, I was falling apart on the inside. I cannot help but wonder how many people could respond to a traumatic situation with such composure. What caused her to display such a calm demeanor? I wonder whether an earlier experience that she encountered had impacted her composure.

Just about a year prior to this tragedy, the same close friend and her now-deceased husband left their daughter and 3-month-old grandchild at home and went to the store. Upon their return, they heard the granddaughter crying. They went upstairs to the daughter's room, where they found her lifeless body with the baby in her arms. I assisted with both funeral arrangements and eulogized both the daughter and husband of my friend. How does one rationalize and cope with such vicissitudes of life? How does one rationalize these horrific life-changing incidents? If you apply the principles of statistics and the laws of probability, I believe that it would be unlikely for these two incidents to occur in the same person's life, and only a year apart.

As I supported my friend in the healing process, I could not help but perceive insurmountable emotional turmoil associated with the process. The gamut of emotions such as grief, denial, stress, pain, and fear, were all manifested in my friend's response to these unfortunate occurrences. In the midst of the grieving process, I visited my friend at her residence on several occasions. During these visits, I observed different individuals attempting to offer words of consolation. I considered some of these individuals as miserable comforters, putting it mildly. They were very generous with their words of consolation and would not take time to listen to what my friend wished to express. I recall having to interject at one point and asked everyone to exercise restraint and allow my grieving friend to express herself in the way she saw fit. What words of encouragement can you give to someone who is experiencing such a degree of trauma?

You may have heard the story about the dejected man who decided to eat his last ripe banana with the intention of ending his life afterward. This is probably a fable, but the moral of the story provides a good life lesson. This man was having a really hard time struggling to survive. He had very limited resources left and it was about to be depleted once he consumed his last banana. He thought that the pressures of life had become unbearable for him at this point. He packed his last banana and a rope in his bag. He then climbed a tree and ate the banana. He dropped the banana peel on the ground below him. He proceeded to tie one end of the rope to a branch of the tree and placed the other end of the rope around his neck with the intention of hanging himself. When he took one last look around before closing his eyes a final time, to his amazement, someone approached the vicinity of the tree, picked up the banana peel, and ate it. He removed the rope from his neck, descended the tree, and went home. This man intended to end his life because of his challenging circumstances, only to realize that there was someone else facing a worse dilemma. If not confronted appropriately, your challenges will isolate you and plague you with a plethora of irrational thoughts. You have to find a way of preventing your trials from causing your demise. Develop a mindset to roll with the punches and remain hopeful for a better day.

Dissatisfactions

During my youthful years, I felt invincible. I thought that I had full control over the direction that my life's journey would take. I was told that hard work is the key to success. I believed that if I worked hard enough and maintained a positive attitude, then I could accurately predict the outcome of my efforts. I was convinced that if I had planned my life well, everything I aspired after would be realized and this would be accomplished in my projected timeframe. It did not take me too long during the young adulthood leg of my journey to realize that, even though the roads along which I traveled were paved with good intentions, the harsh realities of hard knocks, detours, dissatisfactions, and unpredictability were inevitable. If you intend to maintain your sanity and focus, you will have to face and embrace the good and the bad that life imposes upon you.

There will be good days, and there will be bad days. There will be pleasant circumstances, and there will be unpleasant circumstances. There will be desirable and undesirable occurrences. You should anticipate and prepare to encounter a mixture of positives and negatives along life's journey. If you come to terms with the imminence of anxieties, vulnerabilities, limitations, strengths, challenges, and opportunities, then you will feel less pressured to pretend that things are always going well when you are faced with these hurdles. You are not the only one who will face hills and valleys in life. We all have to travel that path. Face it with grace and optimism.

I can understand the apprehension in your willingness to expose your vulnerabilities. You might have done so in the past, and others judged you by your circumstances. You will sometimes share your weaknesses, limitations and challenges in life, and others will decide to define you based on your limitations. I have had the experience of sharing certain personal challenges, and I was judged based on what I divulged. This is insincerity on the part of the perpetrator because we all have vulnerabilities with which we have to contend. We all have struggles. We all have mountains. We all have valleys. We all have undesirable situations that we have to deal with in our lives. It does not matter how calculated or proactive we are, falling off the track is a part of the journey. Some of the greatest men and women of renown who have ever lived, people who impacted the world in very significant ways, were faced with insurmountable challenges, but they kept their eyes on the prize and forge ahead bearing the impact of their hardships.

Overthinking

Some people tend to overthink and over evaluate whatever they encounter in life, while others view every encounter in life with intensity and trepidation. Some people refrain from taking time to stop and smell the roses while traveling along life's journey, while others avoid the roses because of the thorns. It is important to develop the capacity to effectively deal with the pressures of life, and simultaneously enjoy the gifts of life. Some individuals allow their untamed ambition to drive them towards the cliff of disappointment, hopelessness, and insanity. Others are so laid back that they miss their chances to capitalize on great life-changing opportunities that cross their path. Many years ago, I had a conversation with a grown man who lived his adult life, up to that point, in a single room that he rented from his landlord. He had to share certain facilities such as bathroom, kitchen, and living room amenities with other grown men who also rented a room at that same location. One day, he told me that he needed only one plate, one spoon, and one fork because he only catered for himself. You can become so secured in your pond that you fail to venture out into the ocean. Life should not be oversimplified, and neither should one become overwhelmed by its complexities.

If you really are a resilient and ambitious person and you want to do well for yourself, you will seek to press forward despite the obstacles. If you are a caring person, you will care about the people who come under the sphere of your influence. You will be considerate of people who are faced with challenging circumstances. You will seek to make the world a better place for those around you, even in times of your greatest needs; however, you should establish limits and boundaries. In my earlier days, I felt that I was so invincible. I thought that I could always assist those in need, contend with their concerns, and ensure that they overcome their circumstances. I found that sometimes I would become so intimately associated with others' needs to the extent that I essentially assumed the responsibility to secure a desirable resolution to their problems. You might be well intentioned in your attempt to repair the breach in people's lives but be mindful that you cannot save the world. Be warned!

In my field of study, I learned the concepts of entanglement and disengagement. Entanglement is basically becoming ensnared in a human web of interpersonal dysfunctionalities. Disengagement is the ability to address the existing situation without becoming overwhelmed by it. I realized early in adulthood that life has many bumps and not every situation faced by others warrants a savior. I also realized that the outcomes of adversities are not always perfect. If you aspire after greatness, it is impossible for you to go through life unscratched. You should not make it your mission to enable other people's dysfunctions, and neither should you commit to fixing their every problem. You could be found guilty of interrupting some vital teachable moments. Be careful how much you indulge in other people's affairs. I discovered that the more liberal you are in your support of others, the greater the chances of you being taken for granted. You should strive to maintain your focus on your dreams in the face of competing hardships. Your constant yearning and willingness to rescue others can become addictive and distract you from paying attention to your personal needs and significant relationships. Do not become preoccupied with other people's difficulties. They will get through it over time and on their own account. It is very important for you to prioritize your personal affairs and give them your undisrupted attention, irrespective of the inevitable distractions that you will face.

Personal Responsibility

You should face the challenges that life places on your table, and not attempt to avoid them, because they are necessary and inescapable. Whenever you encounter them, you should face them with a positive attitude and a winning anticipation. Irrespective of how many people you have around you, or how many loyal friends and associates you have at your disposal, you are the only one that is vested with the responsibility to handle matters relating to your personal life. Those in your physical and mental space may lend support, but you basically have to personally face whatever life presents you. You hardly, if ever, will find anyone to assume responsibility for your personal affairs, and you should never attempt to manipulate anyone into doing so. Refrain from espousing an attitude that expects others to become the source for replenishment of your resources. A life of dependency will cause you to become a socialized villain, and it is only a matter of time before your antics will result in your demise. You are responsible for the nurturing and growth of every aspect of your life. You have the ultimate obligation to negotiate your survival and advancement. If you embrace the notion of personal responsibility, and demonstrate your willingness to take care of your own business, then your industriousness will be observable, and any essential support that you need will be placed in your path. This is the way our universe functions. Favor is usually gifted to those you expend the effort and endure the process.

You must be prepared to deal with the unpredictable. You can wake up one morning, and everything seems perfect, but as the day progresses, you encounter an unprecedented crisis. It is prudent and highly recommended that you maintain an awareness of the fact of life that bad things do happen to good people. It does not matter how much you name it, claim it, and believe it, you cannot avoid the random or orchestrated trials that life will impose upon you. The most resourceful and proactive human beings are subject to unpleasant surprises. To avoid dejection in the face of hardships, you should embrace the power of positive thinking, and hope for an amicable outcome. There are certain unavoidable hardships that you are destined to face in your lifetime. Your level of maturity and resourcefulness will be manifested in how efficiently you confront and resolve your struggles, while simultaneously maintaining your integrity.

The Unavoidable

Many people act as though they have everything under control, and they behave as though they really have it all together. None of us really have it all together. The truth is that we are all a work in progress. We all have good days and bad days. We arise each day, and some of us muster up the courage to take on life and all that it brings. Some of us either move forward with our routine or we adjust our agenda and embrace our new normal. Others become impatient and intolerant of the unpredictable changes and retreat to a place of self-defeatism. As you deal with life and its quandaries, there will be those on the bleachers who are generous in judging you based on your unfortunate encounters. They will even proceed to put demeaning labels on you. I have come to realize that judgmental people are usually the ones who accumulate a plethora of unbecoming issues in their own lives. They have a tendency to project their own insufficiencies and insecurities on you. Irrespective of how meticulous you are, you will be subjected to the impositions of such personalities, but do not be intimidated by them. Secured people are empathetic and have good intentions towards others. They have a genuine desire to see you rise from the rubble.

Problems will come and problems will go, but you are not defined by your problems. You should see them as stepping stones designed to propel you to heights of greatness in your own life. At no given point in life will everything be exactly as you want it to be. You may have experienced many accomplishments, but that is not an indication that you have been elevated to a status of perfection, or one that absolves you of disappointment or disability. You wake up every day with the potential to face taxing events. The nuances that accompany these events may cause dismal and discouraging disruptions. Do not allow these disruptions to dampen your will to get ahead. If you live long enough, you will realize that the trying situations that confront you are all a part of your growth opportunities. It is important to note that, with every nuance, there is a lesson to be learned and an opportunity to negotiate a desired outcome. You might not necessarily fully grasp the purpose while facing a particular battle, but if you maintain a mindset that there is a reason for the season, you will find the motivation to endure and ultimately conquer. At an opportune time, you will be able to leverage your experience as you seek to climb steeper mountains. You will be able to go into your toolkit of lessons learned and employ a gamut of tools to aid you in your quest to conquer. You were endowed with enriching and empowering life lessons to create exploits. You can make this world a better place by reinvesting in others the rich insights that you gained from dominating and overcoming your hardships. No man is an island and no man stands alone. So, engage the human family and share the victories and expertise that you gained along life's formidable expedition. Someone is waiting to be inspired by you!

People have the tendency to avoid discourses surrounding their own mortality and some seldom ponder the fact that human life is temporary. Our existence on earth has an inescapable expiration date. Relatively few people live beyond the age of 80. Fewer people live beyond the age of 90, and even fewer people live beyond a 100 years. Regardless of your longevity, you are going to expire one day. Medical intervention will prolong one's life, and temporary restoration of health is often realized as a result of scientific interventions; however, everyone eventually dies. It is inevitable that, sooner or later, you will be faced with life-threatening encounters. It is only a matter of time before it is your turn to face your mortality. If you encounter a medical challenge, please take consolation in the fact that you are not alone in such a predicament. This is an unavoidable punctuation in everyone's journey. Your dilemma may cause you to become fearful, and isolated, and you may resort to self-pity. It might become difficult or even intolerable for you to face the inescapability of your termination but be assured that you are not alone. There are many other people going through similar situations. Your departure from this life is an imminent eventuality. In the face of this, I implore you to square your shoulders, take full charge of the remainder of your journey, and start living your best life now!

Purpose

What's your purpose on earth? You have a purpose that extends beyond the confines of your current limitations. Including in your purpose is a mandate to deposit life given sustenance in someone who needs it. The best investment you can make in the human economy is using the equity gained from your tumults and triumphs to positively influence another person's life. One of the ways to influence a person's life is to share lessons learned from your encounters along the journey. Whenever you are faced with teachable moments, be mindful that you are being equipped for the greater good. If you focus on purpose, you will be motivated to embrace the journey and learn the lessons inherent in every setback. You may be inclined to be discouraged whenever you are unable to bring a timely resolution to your challenging circumstance, but time is the master and it will not facilitate a premature culmination. Some of your problems will not have an amicable outcome, and some of your fixable problems will not come to a swift resolution. Some problems will require that you make adjustments to accommodate them for an extended period. You may have to deal with the reality of patiently living through a painful predicament until it runs its long and unpredictable course. Some plights are predestined to remain with you for the duration of your life. Permanency does not imply defeat. In some cases, you are required to face your affliction and make the necessary adjustments to coexist with the condition. This is the mantle imposed upon you and it is designed to make you highly qualified to perform in the arena that requires an elevated dimension of patience and endurance. Some individuals are strapped to a tough test because they need to learn vital lessons that provide an impetus that will help to overcome their difficulty.

In life you must learn to face misfortunes, find a way of effectively negotiating them, and remain committed to your ultimate goals. This is an empowering and transformative response to hard times. Do not agitate over the encroachments on your life. Such a response is counterproductive to your growth and development. There are certain things that you will have to face, and for which you have to actively find a resolution. There are certain things that you will have to personally work towards fixing, and there are certain things that are designed to be unfixable. There are certain things imposed upon you that you will not be able to rectify, so you have to learn to coexist with them. Some people spend their valuable time and expend their priceless energy in trying to repair the unrepairable. This results in wasting of precious time, effort, and mental resources. Do not expend your effort trying to correct something that was not designed to be corrected. Some things are introduced into your life to anchor you, to build up your mental fortitude, and to give you the stamina to face and overcome the new challenges that tomorrow brings. Consider these as indispensable instruments for your survival and domination. The unfamiliar paths, the intimidating hurdles, the deep valleys, and the high mountains are all a part of the preparation process that is designed to point you towards your destiny. Face your obstacles deliberately!

Positivity

When you are confronted with obstacles, you will not always be inclined to face them with enthusiasm. It is normal to approach certain obstacles with trepidation. You may even sometimes approach them with disdain. It is reasonable to entertain concerns for your survival but at the same time you should build the courage to approach your challenges with a growth mindset. Never assume the victim role. Be very measured in how much energy and time you dedicate towards seeking a resolve for a prevailing or recurring obstacle. It might just be there to make you a better person. Seek to identify the good in any situation that you face. Unfortunately, many people spend too much of their time complaining instead of focusing on evaluating and strategizing to manipulate the misfortune to their benefit. There is a biblical principle that states, *"To whom much is given, much is required."* Therefore, it stands to reason that if your purpose in life is enormously significant, then your troubles are going to be equally significant. Your obstacles should be seen as a training ground for future exploits. The more trying the circumstance, the more benefits you will derive, and the more empowered you will be from the lessons learned.

If your trials in life are turbulent and appear to be insurmountable, be assured that inherent in your assignment on earth, is monumental and far reaching influence. If you are enduring frequent seasons of troublesome times, then be assured that you are destined for elevation to the status of an impactful and possibly global influencer. You could very well be in training for promotion from a local to a global force with which to be contended; and age is not a factor in this equation. I believe that some individuals are destined to have a local impact, while others are destined to have a global impact. If you are destined to impact people beyond the boundary of your local environment, then you have to be prepared to be tested and tried to dimensions that will stretch you beyond measure. You cannot arbitrarily venture out and impact people in a significant way if you are oblivious of the grit and grind it takes to confront and conquer. If you possess what it takes to face and eliminate annoying obstacles, then you will be adequately equipped to be assigned to undertake and defeat difficult and disastrous encounters. You must understand and appreciate that if you intend to negotiate and incapacitate the twists and turns of life, you must assume a posture of optimism, persistence, and domination.

You And Others

One major distraction people destined for greatness face is the potential impact that critical observers have on their momentum. There will always be people who judge you based on your misfortunes. People will judge you by the clothes you wear, the source of your employment, the car you drive, and more so by the adversities that you face. If your career goals are not as impressive as those around you, that does not make you a lesser person. You might not be able to demand the salary that those around you enjoy, but that does not make you less significant. No one person is better than the other. We are all human beings on a path to self-actualization. The ultimate goal should be to become the best version of yourself, and help others become the best version of themselves. As you face the challenges that life brings, seek to overcome them with diligence and with precision. Let the harsh judgment that others direct towards you serve as an inspiration instead of an interruption. You should constantly ask yourself how you can use your wealth of experience to propel you towards your destiny, and simultaneously inspire those striving to fulfill their own destiny.

You should derive joy from supporting others and from contributing to their success. There are people around you who crave your encouragement and affirmation. There are people around you who would be grateful for a comforting embrace. There are people around you who desire a verbal expression of love. There are people around you who would be thankful for an occasional hot meal. There are people around you who need a single month's rent to get them through to the next paycheck, and then they will be on track with their essential financial obligations. If you have an appreciation for other people and a concern for their needs, then you should lend a hand whenever the opportunity presents itself. You should constantly seek opportunities to lighten the burden of the less fortunate. Seek out opportunities to be the wind beneath the wings of the less fortunate and inspire them to sore like an eagle. You would probably be shocked to know how little of your personal resources it will take to generate a tsunami of pleasant possibilities for someone in need. If you operate with the understanding that the extension of a helping hand adds hope and civility to human existence, then we will be constantly motivated in our desire to give back to the society that cradles us along our own journey. Help somebody whenever you can, and when you expire you would have left this world a better place.

Challenges

At this juncture in your life, you might be faced with unresolved challenges. If displayed in the public arena, your challenges would probably not only cause you embarrassment, but they may change the perception that others have concerning your character and amiability. People will judge you based on your problems or on the superficiality of what you project, and not on the substance of your character. Do not judge your worth based on public opinion. The weight of your load might tempt you to think less of yourself, but irrespective of your burden, be assured that you are not defined by what befalls you, but by what you inherently represent. Whatever befalls you will either diminish or elevate you. Regardless of the intensity or impact of your difficulty, be mindful that troubles do not last forever. If you have a mindset that your dilemma is permanent, then you may assume a mindset of hopelessness. Your mind can either break you or make you. The absence of hope results in the absence of the will to fight. Keep hope alive and maintain a mindset of positivity.

I believe that when faith does not deliver, then hope becomes your next most potent defense. Have you ever been faced with a predicament where, even thou you put in the time and the effort and exercised your faith for an expected outcome, you discovered that the anticipated outcome was not realized? Like many other people, you were probably conflicted over the fact that you followed the prescribed success formula but did not get the predicted result. In such trying times it is important to be reminded that a roadblock is not a terminus. A roadblock should propel you to become creative in your thinking, inventive in your imagination, and extensive in your alternatives. There is never a single way or means of reaching your destination. If the road is blocked, do not sit and wait indefinitely for it to be cleared. The blocked road may never be cleared under your watch, or on your timetable. Some roadblocks may even be designed to last for the duration of your life span to protect you from some impending danger. Make an assessment and, if necessary, find an alternate route and continue to move in the direction of your destination. Jump over the fence, climb the steep mountain, swim across the river, but keep on moving. If you are unable to swim, then build a raft. There might be crocodiles in the water but be undeterred by obstacles and pending dangers. Your destiny is your mandate. Let nothing stand between you and your destiny. Be fearless and unperturbed in your pursuit of purpose. By all credible means, do whatever you need to do in order to accomplish your mission on earth. Neglect is not an option!

There are many incredibly worthwhile things in life that I have accomplished. I had no clue how I was going to accomplish some of them. At the outset, I did not have the necessary resources to accomplish some of my ambitious dreams, but I nonetheless kept hope alive and forged ahead. You have the energy within you to light a fire under your feet and the potential to leap towards your destination. Sometimes you have to fan your own flames because those around you may not believe in your ability to accomplish the things you set out to achieve. Develop a mental map of what you hope to accomplish in life and let it guide you to the finish line. Keep a journal of what you set out to undertake at each stage of your journey and then repeatedly verbalize it to yourself. Do so repeatedly with conviction and fervor. Say the things that are not yet apparent as though they were already accomplished. Say it whether or not those around you believe it. You have to keep saying and believing it to yourself. Remain persistent and undeterred in your aspirations and consistently confront the challenges with uncompromising determination to succeed.

Do not allow people to intimidate you into changing your ambitious goals and positive perspective on life. In moments of doubt and disappointment, and there will be those moments, walk out on the stage of life with courage and determination. There will be times when the conditions for battle do not appear ideal, but there is no perfect condition or time for you to venture out on the frontiers of life as you walk towards your destiny. You will not always be inclined to engage in a passionate pursuit. The best time to venture out is now. You will be better able to win your battles and positively impact those around you when you proceed without hesitation, despite the tumults. You should be the intimidator instead of the intimidated. Some of your wishes will come true and some may not. Some of your plans will materialize and some may not; however, be confident in the fact that every step you take in the right direction counts towards the evolution of your mission and the realization of your vision. Swim against the current!

Points to Ponder

    a. Anticipate

        i. Have an understanding that there will be obstacles along the way

        ii. Have an expectation to personally face obstacles along the way

        iii. Be prepared to confront obstacles along the way

    b. Evaluate

        i. Investigate the obstacle to determine its substance

        ii. Examine the obstacle to determine its intensity

        iii. Assess the obstacle to determine whether it is repairable

    c. Accommodate

        i. Be decisive with your approach in dealing with the obstacle

        ii. Discount obstacles you determine are not worth your attention

        iii. Confront obstacles you determine are worth your attention

    d. Initiate

        i. Identify alternatives in dealing with the obstacle

        ii. Choose the most practical alternatives in dealing with the obstacle

        iii. Implement the chosen alternatives in tackling the obstacle

e. Commemorate

 i. Acknowledge your accomplishment in conquering the obstacle

 ii. Appreciate yourself and those who assist you in conquering the obstacle

 iii. Celebrate your accomplishment in conquering every obstacle

Challenges are inevitable in the grand scheme of things. It's the way we respond to them that shapes our identity, illuminates our path, and thrusts us towards our destiny."

Reflections

Chapter 9

Keep Moving Forward
Forge Ahead With Toughness And Determination

★ ★ ★

Misfortune is a potentially potent tool. It is the way we apply the lessons learned from our calamities that determines our degree of maturity. We should take our focus off where we 'fell' and place it on where we 'slipped.' Our mishaps should be seen as teachable moments that are designed for us to emerge equipped from our enclaves of despair. Teachable moments should be used to analyze how we executed in the past and inform how to move forward. They should arm us with knowledge to guide our steps towards significant growth and development.

Take Charge

The strength of your resilience determines your ability to bounce back from misfortunes. It is your ability to forge ahead, in spite of the presenting circumstances, which determines your sustainability. It is your willingness to keep on moving ahead, despite the obstacles that disrupt your routine, which determines the rate of your progression. Resilience is really the ability to rise above the rubble. It is the intestinal fortitude to push ahead, in spite of opposing forces, which builds your character. It is easier said than done. People who offer guidance often tend to underestimate how difficult it is to apply their prescription when the victim is under duress. When you are on the outside looking in, the matter may appear to be easily resolvable; but when you are actually in the midst of a turmoil, the proposed resolutions oftentimes appear to be unattainable. Onlookers should be mindful of the fact that when one is in the midst of a crisis, the perceived intensity is oftentimes exaggerated. When lending support to people, it is advisable to avoid being dogmatic on how to deal with the matter at hand. Imposing your personal advice is really enabling people to look outside of themselves for a resolution. It is an intrusion on people's personal responsibility to dictate to them how they should handle their personal affairs. We are custodians for our own affairs, and therefore it is our responsibility to make our own decisions and to bear the consequences of the outcome. Take charge of your business!

When a person is faced with an issue and needs to make a decision, the intervener's role is to offer insights in identifying alternative ways of resolving the matter at hand. When the person identifies the alternative approaches in dealing with the issue, the intervener should then offer guidance in helping the person to determine the pros and the cons of each alternative. After this step is taken, a personal decision should then be made in choosing an alternative, based on the most beneficial option. Once this is done, the person is obligated to take ownership of both the decision and the outcome. People need to take responsibility for their affairs, and be given the opportunity and guidance in making and owning their own decisions. This approach will allow them to own the responsibility for resolving their challenges and avoid the inclination to depend on others to make decisions for their personal lives. If you give advice on how to solve a person's problem, and the outcome is undesirable, then you will be culpable if the outcome is undesirable. Avoid telling people how to solve their problems and encourage them to take charge of their own concerns.

Take Responsibility

Be intentional in guiding people to become independent thinkers. This quality will ensure that they are accountable for their own actions. If you find yourself in a position that requires you to assist those dealing with challenges, be diligent in not imposing your personal opinions, neither should you dictate your own resolution. People have a tendency to offer guidance based on their personal experiences. We are coming from diverse family dynamics and cultural backgrounds which influence our outlook on life; therefore, we should be diligent in not providing solutions which are void of contextual compatibility. The formula that was employed in resolving your issues might not work for someone else. So, as you assist people in moving forward with their lives, be sure to steer away from the imposition of your subjective opinions and approaches.

Some people are inclined to remain in a state of inaction and assign others the responsibility of dictating how they should navigate their lives. It is irresponsible for you to surrender your personal responsibilities to others, and allow others to dictate the steps that you should take in handling your affairs. If you do so, then you are actually relinquishing the responsibility of your stewardship to others. You are accountable for your life, and by that token you are accountable for your decisions and actions. It is desirable for others to provide you with moral support along the way, but ultimately make it your point of duty to make and own your choices. An independent attitude is a virtue that should be cultivated, demonstrated, and embraced.

At some point along your journey, you will feel overwhelmed and without a sense of direction. During these trying times, you should not lose the will to manage your choices. Irrespective of how strong or how prepared you think you are in taking on life, you will be faced with formidable obstructions. Irrespective of how many strategic plans you put together to forge ahead in life, you are going to have some bumps in the road. You are going to have some life-altering disappointments. You are going to be faced with some unpredictable setbacks that will have no rational explanations. You are going to be imposed upon by those individuals whose intentions are to distract you and interrupt your journey. You should adopt a warrior stance and claim your territory. You have the right and accountability to detonate anything that stands in the way of your progress.

You might be on the verge of accomplishing your attainable goals, and out of nowhere, someone enters your life and disrupts your plan. There may be sadistic people around you who will turn the road sign in the wrong direction and create chaos. What will you do with these distractions? How can you turn these lemons into lemonade? How will you rise from the rubble? You may become despondent and incline to give up. You may lose your will to continue moving forward. You may attempt to fight back, but after no evidence of compelling result, you may become tired of trying. You may want to give up on your goals and aspirations. You will have to find what it takes from within to step away from the noise of distraction and remind yourself of what initially motivated you to commence the journey. You are the author of your plans and so you have the freedom to revisit and redirect your affairs. So, never give up when your journey becomes confusing. Step back for a while and recalibrate. Whatever you are faced with in life, never allow it to derail you. Step up to the plate and look within yourself for a solution. Take ownership of your encounters and be unyielding in moving forward!

Look Ahead

Everything around you may appear to be normal in the eyes of your admirers and observers. Your physical appearance might be impeccable and you might be functioning effectively in the marketplace. You may represent the picture of progress from all indications, but when you get home to your secluded space, the impact of the exasperating circumstances of life overwhelms you. You might be afraid to go to bed and afraid to wake up in the morning. This is unquestionably the representation of an unhealthy way of living. One alternative in dealing with this impasse is to just sit and do nothing about it while life passes you by. That is an unadvisable alternative in addressing such critical crisis. In times of adversity, you have got to look deep down in the recesses of your heart and unearth an enduring desire to move forward. With this desire, lift up your eyes and look ahead with hope and determination to dominate anything that crosses your path. The moment you stop trying is the moment you start dying. In the human scheme of things, if you stop looking ahead and refrain from moving forward, then you are diminishing. If you recommit to your resolve to succeed and reinvigorate your effort to advance, then you will once again be on track. Stagnation is the nemesis of advancement.

There will be moments in time, based on the presenting state of affairs, that you will be unable to move your agenda forward. It is important for you to recognize that these moments are temporary.

When you are faced with episodes of inaction, devise a strategy that will keep you moving on the spot. Moving on the spot prevents inaction and promotes exploration. Do an inventory of your life while moving on the spot. Evaluate your journey while moving on the spot. Make meaningful adjustments to your plans while moving on the spot. Never sit down and wait for something to happen. Think of new ideas, new strategies, new hobbies, new opportunities, and new methodologies. Just keep moving and look ahead! There will be times when you have to simply stay in position and clear your mind; and that is in order. When you stop moving and thinking, your life tends to spiral out of control and takes you down the self-destructive path that leads to the demolition of your desires. There are so many people in our society today, more than you will ever imagine, who are at their wits' end and not sure how to reboot. When faced with such a dismal disposition, take consolation in the fact that unfortunate occurrences often lead to avenues of boundless opportunities. Every impediment that you face carries with it the possibility of new horizons.

You may lose the job that sustains you, or the career that you have invested in all your life may come to an abrupt end. You may be in danger of losing your home after honoring your mortgage obligations for many years. When these major misfortunes occur in your life, it is time to seek alternative means of moving forward. Could it be that the security of your job is harnessing you to obligations that are no longer aligned with the direction in which your journey is propelling you? Some of the things with which you wrestle were introduced in your life only as a transient step along the journey towards your destiny. Your comfort zone is a conspiracy against your evolution and the actualization of your calling in life. The rug is sometimes pulled from beneath us because we have settled in a state which was only meant to be transient.

Could it be that things are shaking up around you so that you will be forced to look ahead towards more monumental undertakings? That job that you have lost might be the best thing that ever happened to you. It could be the impetus that you need to initiate your strides towards your supreme purpose. How about using the time you have at your disposal during your destabilized state to develop ideas into an action plan or to revisit and revamp your career goals? Could it be that the perceived losses that you are mourning were no longer aligned with your evolved value system and your enriched abilities? You may have lost your house because it is time that you relocate to a new environment that provides better opportunities that are in alignment with your aspirations. Nothing happens just by chance. The prodding of the universe is purposeful, and if you allow yourself to be guided by it, then everything that transpires in your life will translate into the attainment of your highest purpose on earth. The twists and turns of your journey might be uncomfortable, but inherent in every process is a seed that is waiting to germinate and flourish into inconceivable opportunities and rewards.

You were born with the genetic material for a personalized intent called destiny. Everything that happens in your life is thrusting you towards your destiny. You are placed on the face of the earth for a mission, and you need to accomplish that mission before you leave the earth. For the duration of your lifespan, you have been vested with the task of making a tangible contribution to society. You should constantly keep that in mind and persistently seek to position yourself for your purpose. Like everyone else, your life has an expiration date. Spend your time productively because you do not know how much time is allotted for you to complete your earthly assignment. You do not want to spend the last days of your tenure on earth pondering over whether you have accomplished your purpose. Regrets should not be on your plate when you approach the end of your journey. March forward!

Balance

In order to move ahead and progress efficiently, your life has to be balanced in all aspects. People sometimes find themselves in a bind because they are out of balance. They might be doing well in the physical dimension but are not doing as well in the mental dimension. They might be doing well in the physical and mental dimensions but are not doing as well in the spiritual dimension. They might be doing well in the physical, mental, and spiritual dimensions but doing poorly in the social dimension. They might not be experiencing a fulfilled social life, and boredom becomes a prominent part of their existence. A friend once inquired of me what the outcome would be if we were balanced in some of these dimensions but deficient in others. My response was that our existence would be out of equilibrium. We tend to overcompensate in the dimensions which we master and neglect the ones in which we are deficient. An imbalanced life results in people living below their potential. You cannot live your best life when things are out of equilibrium. Pay attention to the functioning of all the dimensions of your life.

A dysfunctional person loses momentum and lease on life, and this opens the door to negative energy. Negative energy breeds depression, disorientation, and demotivation. The managing of your life is your obligation. You are not as mentally, emotionally, and physically fortified as you may think. Your mind and emotions, if not handled with care, have the potential to destabilize you. They can take you to undesirable places and incapacitate you. They can take you to dark and crippling places. They can take you to places you never dreamt you would go. If the circumstances of life take you to unfamiliar places, it is important that you swiftly recognize your misplacement; and you have to recognize, admit, and reveal to those who have your best interests at heart that you are not doing well. Do not give your significant others the impression that you are fine when you are not. If you need help, then get it. Do not allow yourself to become grounded by your problems. If you ever found yourself in a place of despair, do not remain in such a place. Be courageous and take the initiative in securing the help you need to get you back on track. Acknowledge whatever is placed on your plate and deal with it!

I implore you to check in on your friends and loved ones and investigate whether they are doing well. You should be very observant in this regard. You have to be discerning because your friends or loved ones may be overwhelmed with life threatening crises, and you miss the signs that they are in trouble. Your support might be all the resource that is needed. All they need to survive might be a warm embrace and the reassurance that everything is going to be alright. They may also need to know that the path they are on is familiar to others, and they are not the only ones dealing with such predicaments. You have had your fair share of obstacles along the way so this could be an opportune time for you to use the power of empathy and provide assistance. You should never be apprehensive in reaching out and helping those for whom you care, especially when you are aware that they are faced with roadblocks along the way. It is unacceptable for you to go silent when your loved ones are facing adversities. They may not necessarily need your financial resources. All they may need is a little of your time and a listening ear. In assisting someone in distress, learn to listen more than you talk. Those in distress need the assurance that someone is listening and understanding the horrors with which they are contending. Remain observant of your surroundings because you may be the lifeline for someone's survival. As you move ahead in life, be mindful of those who need your support in their quest to regain their desire and strength to reset and get ahead.

Support

You would be surprised to know that there are people around you who are experiencing severely difficult times, but you could never tell by their appearance. If you practice to look beyond the facade, you will likely find a lonely friend who is pining after some attention in hope of gaining support to negotiate their struggles. You should not judge the emotional health of your friends based on a smiling countenance, a jovial spirit, or material success. It does not matter how much material possession people may have, the time will come when they will need some moral support to tide them over a boisterous sea of issues. You cannot save the world, but to a certain extent, you should hold yourself somewhat accountable for the security of those who you really care about. You should assist your loved ones to rise from the dust of dejection and get beyond the circumstances that yoke them to their distress. You should provide them assurance and support so that they can have a fighting chance in making it through the storms of life. Be prepared to persuade them to the point where they will once again uplift themselves and move forward towards their destiny.

Navigating life is not easy for the young and neither is it easy for the old. It can actually be remarkably challenging for the older population. Teenagers and young adults may look at older persons and assume that they are quite comfortable, and at peace with that phase of their lives. They do so not realizing that older persons often wrestle with the realities associated with aging. No one gets to rehearse a particular phase of life prior to experiencing it. Consider a 60-year-old or a 70-year-old person who has gone through physical and mental changes in life. Physical and mental changes can be either drastic or progressive. With aging also comes the possibility of significant health challenges. The pain of a broken heart can become more intense as one advance in age. The reality of unrealized dreams and broken promises marinate throughout life, and if not reconciled, tend to surface as one ages. Death and dying become more impending. Some people do not age as gracefully as others and this can create insecurity for some. The aging population has all of these daunting certainties with which to contend. It is difficult to deal with these unplanned certainties without an effective support system. Taking these things into consideration, you should aspire to get beyond shallow interactions and engage in the building of sustainable relationships. This will definitely come in handy as you advance in age. Seek a friend before you need one!

You should seek to establish amicable and lasting relationships. Some people find it challenging to establish relationships because they are oriented to believe that relationship is synonymous to intimacy. As a school teacher, I taught an eighth grade social studies class on the subject of the community. I was focusing on relationships building when I realized that some of my students were of the impression that relationship was synonymous with intimacy. I was compelled to clarify the matter. Relationship building without a connotation of intimacy can be of great value, irrespective of the age group. Be sure to establish compatible social relationships with your peers and others with common interests. Your circle gets small with age, so you should seek to cultivate healthy and sustainable relationships, so that you are assured of peer support as you advance in age. Join organizations and community groups with people of common values and interests. You can maintain a fulfilled lifestyle at any age. If you have been around for a few decades, I can assure you that you will find individuals with common interests, common experiences, and common aspirations. Start renovating your relationship portfolio now!

Take control of your happiness and do not allow anyone to control or negatively impact it. Some people unfortunately allow others to control their happiness. There are individuals who have allowed people who are already dead to control their happiness. In other instances, individuals allow people who are no longer in their lives to control their emotions, and ultimately their happiness. You have to shake yourself from the impact of past negative experiences, dismiss thoughts of revenge and remorse, and look ahead to brighter days. I was once told that wanting revenge on someone is like you drinking poison and expecting the object of your vengeance to die. The greatest revenge is for you to reconfigure your journey and soar to heights of incredible attainment in all aspects of your life. Let nothing stand in the way of your ability to live your best life. It is never too late for a shower of rain. It is never too late for you to pick yourself up and to move forward in your quest to fulfill your heart's desires. Age is not a factor in accomplishing your goals. Stand up, be thankful for your life, and love yourself strongly, because hardly anyone will love you more than how much you love your own self. Adversity does not give you license to resign yourself to a dreary existence and it should not cause you to abandon your desire to live your best life now. Do not ever pause or give up on your quest to live a fulfilled life! Forge ahead with toughness and determination!

Points to Ponder

a. Have a movement mindset

   i. Avoid inaction

   ii. Always be willing to move forward

   iii. Look for opportunities to generate action

b. Investigate the possibilities

   i. Look for new doors when the current ones refuse to open

   ii. Consider unorthodox alternatives

   iii. Be willing to take feasible chances and do not vacillate

c. Equip to counteract

   i. Refuse to stagnate when faced with obstacles

   ii. Identify next steps while combating existing obstacles

   iii. Decide on the most appropriate moves while contending with obstacles

d. Take action

   i. Accept the need for the next move while combating the obstacles

   ii. Disregard obstacles that are insignificant

   iii. Activate the appropriate next step while confronting the obstacle

e. Endure

   i.   Be courageous in the midst of difficulties

  ii.   Remain expectant amidst difficulties

 iii.   Let failures serve to propel you

You are the product of both your failures and your successes. To agitate over the unfortunate occurrences in your life is to be ungrateful towards the diverse and varied realities that serve to elevate you to your current position.

Reflections

_____

_____

_____

_____

_____

_____

_____

_____

_____

_____

_____

_____

_____

_____

_____

_____

_____

_____

Chapter 10

The School Of Experience

Experiences Are Teachable Moments To Benefit You

* ★ *

Life's experiences are a cocktail of bitter and sweet, and you must acquire the taste in order to embrace and enjoy your existence. The caliber of a compelling experience extends beyond the limits of knowledge acquisition and the grasping of concepts, to the undertaking of complex challenges, finding feasible solutions; and simultaneously acquiring practical and sustainable life skills, personal growth, and continuous development.

Education

Experience is the greatest teacher in life. Just as how students in the classroom are instructed and evaluated, our experiences instruct and evaluate us. I like project-based learning. It is an instructional method that delivers the instruction, and then the knowledge gained is used to solve real-world problems. Application is the key. You have to apply the content. The highest-earning individuals are those who are critical thinkers, those who are able to solve complex problems, and those who meritoriously apply their knowledge. Life provides the learner with the opportunity to learn. Experience equips the learner with tools to apply the knowledge gained. Experience is equitable. It provides growth opportunities for all. The education gained by experience is beneficial to us only if we apply it at the appropriate time for the appropriate reason.

Our life is a story, and we are constantly narrating our story on the stage of life; we are also the author, director, and sole performer. A clear understanding of the crucial role that both positive and negative experiences contribute to our growth will bring a certain degree of consolation and clarity of purpose. It will eradicate trepidation and regrets. It will also help us to remain resolute as we move through phases of uncertainty and unpredictability. We are all placed on the face of the earth for a specific purpose. It is important to note that our destiny is predetermined; therefore, we should not exert our energy trying to control it. There are aspects of the journey over which we have control, but our destiny is essentially prepackaged. Our responsibility is to manage the journey. Each of us is placed on the face of the earth for a particular reason, and it is our responsibility to manage and capitalize on the opportunities that are presented to us in every season. Many of us spend an inordinate amount of time trying to control the circumstances around us. We expend so much energy trying to control these situations, not realizing that certain interferences are placed in our paths for our own good. Pressure and stress are building blocks for upward mobility. These growth opportunities are natural to our very existence, and if we take the correct approach in dealing with them, the outcome will be rewarding.

Your growth and maturity are determined by your competence to navigate life, your capability to deal with the pitfalls, and your capacity to roll with the punches. What you need to come to terms with, for this journey, is the disquieting fact that you were not handed a blueprint. If you were given a blueprint to reference along your journey, then whenever confronted with a conundrum, you would be able to scrutinize the blueprint and ascertain a prescribed response. Conversely, you were provided a compass in your arsenal. A compass is not a meal handed to you on the platter or a prescription that dictates a remedy. It provides you with a general direction to keep you on track and leads you in the right direction. You have to facilitate the navigation. You have to put forth some effort. You have to do some heavy lifting. At best, life will instruct you on how to leverage the added value of the experiences that you gained along your journey.

Most people address their challenges based on the experiences that they garnered along their journey. Experience is a very powerful tool. We all have one kind of experience or another. Some people are inclined to play it safe and others are inclined to avoid the risks; therefore, the strength of their experience is not compelling enough to inform the caliber resolution that is required to advance their cause. If you always play it too safe, you will be at a disadvantage when faced with crisis situations. If you are practical, pragmatic, and adventurous, you will be guaranteed a substantial number of both good and bad experiences. It is consoling to note that both good and bad experiences play a vital role in how we tackle and overcome our setbacks. As the steward of your journey, you may be inclined to spend much of your time trying to control the situations around you; however, it is important to remember that there are many things in life over which you have no control. You were deliberately not assigned the responsibility to exert control over the things which are placed in your life to build you up. You do not have the power to control everything that happens in your life. You should be mindful of how much energy you exert in an effort to avoid unpreventable steps along your journey. Roll with the punches!

Perception

Your experiences impact your perception, and your perception is a hundred percent reality to you. It is, therefore, important that you entertain healthy perceptions. Unfortunately, the clarity of your reality could be distorted by your subjective analysis and unhealthy responses to your experiences. What do you derive from your experiences? Many divorcees remarry, and whenever the new spouse displays a particular behavior, it is perceived as a replication of the undesirable qualities of the former spouse. It does not matter how pure the motives of this new spouse are, they trigger a red flag. You have to be very careful how you allow your past experiences to color your judgment. It is important that you evaluate your perception regularly. Based on past experiences we are all subjected to a certain level of prejudice, but we should be careful not to allow the past to dampen the prospects of the present or threaten the fruitfulness of the future.

Your perceptions can be inaccurate at best and unfounded at worst. You have to be acutely aware of the fact that perceptions, which are usually influenced by past experiences, do color responses. Your perceptions are sometimes influenced by your acquired prejudices. Your perception drives your expectations. Your expectations influence your attitude, and your attitude impacts your outcome. If your perception is inaccurate, then it could alter the intended outcome. People often conjure up in their minds how they are going to respond to a particular situation, and this is based on their sensitivities; hence, you should become aware of your biases and never allow them to stand in the way of your progress.

Be aware that on any given day you are dealing with people who are victims of their circumstances. People show up with all that they represent, including their baggage. Consequently, you should take all the variables into account, and remain objective at all times, when dealing with people. This will minimize the potential for unnecessary confrontations, unpleasant surprises, and emotional rollercoasters. Have you ever anticipated a particular outcome, only to discover that it did not come to fruition? Inaccurate perceptions can distort your focus and hinder your ability to establish meaningful interactions. Do not allow your perception to interrupt your opportunities or prevent your progress.

Choose Your Battles

Choose your battles. If you have a healthy outlook on life, you will not be easily triggered by unfavorable responses. You will also not be easily offended by negative responses and noxious energies. Sometimes people will avoid articulating or displaying exactly how they feel, but that does not prevent their negative energy from creating a repulsive climate. In order to maintain your composure in awkward social settings, you should learn how to deflect negativity in all its manifestations. It is important for you to possess the necessary emotional intelligence to counteract inappropriate impositions, while simultaneously maintaining a positive spirit. When others deal inappropriately with you, it is none of your business. It has nothing to do with you but it has everything to do with them. I was once facilitating a meeting, and one of the participants interrupted the meeting to make a point. I thought that the person was planning on endorsing the meeting agenda. I was shocked when I realized that the person disrupted the meeting only to confront me personally concerning a matter that was unrelated to the meeting agenda. I allowed the person to vent, and then I told the participants that we would now proceed with the meeting. I gave no credence to the inappropriate interjection. You should by all means avoid fueling the fire of conflict.

People make judgments about you, about others, and about situations. These judgments are based on their personal experiences, suppositions, and emotional states. People will judge you wrongly, and provide indefensible justifications for their unscrupulous actions. Some offenders even share their unwarranted indictments with their associates and sympathizers. There are always gullible individuals, including some of your own associates, who will buy into the disparagement and judge you based on false allegations. Do not be surprised if some who you consider as your associate downgrade their impression of you based on unsubstantiated points of view. Do not get in the habit of explaining your side of the story. It is hardly likely that your explanation will impact the unsubstantiated opinions of disloyal people. If you are the victim of wrongful allegations, it is important that you remain steadfast in your strides as you anticipate your vindication. Once you are assured of your innocence, you should not allow counterproductive forces to dampen your spirit. In the same token, you should be careful how you judge others by what was imparted to you by character assassinators. Give others a chance to prove themselves to you and never color your perception of them based on heresy. You should be intentional in giving people a chance to prove themselves. You may one day require the same sentiment. Guard your perceptions.

Trust

Life will give you some amazing experiences, and it will also give you some horrible ones. People will breach your trust and leave you feeling betrayed, but never allow yourself to flounder in defeat. Never allow upsetting experiences to prevent you from building meaningful relationships. You might be apprehensive in establishing relationships in fear that they might not be sustained. With this mindset, if you are not careful, you will always find indicators to confirm your fear. This is self-induced insecurity that will hamper your ability to develop and maintain meaningful interactions. Healthy relationships can only be forged when you sustain a reasonable expectation of others. People tend to rise or fall to the level of your expectation. You have to maintain your belief in humanity. There are some unreasonable people among us, but there are also some reasonable ones. Do not live with the anticipation that everyone who walks into your life will eventually hurt you. Some people have good intentions for you and, if given a chance, they will engage and uplift you.

Do not allow your apprehensions to deprive you of the opportunities to pursue meaningful relationship building. Do not harness yourself to pessimism. Could it be that you are standing in the way of your ability to build sustainable relationships? You have to give people a chance to prove themselves. Remember, you cannot control your destiny; you can only manage it. So, bottom line, you have to manage your own relationship expectation, and rationalize your assumptions. It might seem safe to isolate yourself from people, especially if you have endured painful experiences. Be careful to avoid negatively stereotyping persons whose presence in your life could be mutually beneficial. Some of the proudest people that I know project themselves as being humble, and some of the humblest people I know were initially perceived as being prideful. We should be careful to address each situation based on its own merits.

As a young teenager, I once shook the hand of a young lady, and she scolded me for holding on to her hand for too long. I did not consciously do so, and I certainly had no ulterior motive for holding on to her hand. I am not sure why she reacted in that manner, but I believe that this encounter triggered something from her past. My relationship with that young lady was never the same. I was subsequently incredibly cautious when interacting with her. It is important to note that, for a long time, this experience caused me to be extremely careful when giving handshakes. You can disrupt a potentially good situation if you allow the effects of past incidents dictate your reaction. You can become your own worst enemy if you allow the past to impose on your present functioning. You have to let things go. You might have had some bad episodes with people. You might have been deceived by individuals who you thought meant you well, or you might have been the victim of an abusive relationship. You should be careful not to allow these harsh realities to eliminate the possibility of you nurturing meaningful and lasting affiliations.

In dealing with the encroachments of life, be intentional in challenging yourself to frequently revisit how you relate to others and analyze how your biases influence your actions and inactions. The outcome of this informative exercise should inform your future responses to matters regarding relationship building. The outcome of your dealings with people will either be constructive or destructive, depending on your objectivity in analyzing each scenario. If you harbor grudges, resentment, and lack of forgiveness, please be aware that your past is holding you hostage. You cannot allow yourself to be held captive indefinitely because of the scars from the past. Do not allow your progress to be inhibited by people from your past. If that is the case then they are still in control of your life. You should be the only one with jurisdiction over the way you live your life. Who is holding you hostage? Who is controlling your responses? You should be your own primary influencer. Trust your intuitions and take charge!

Control

Many people are controlled by others. This manipulation is sometimes achieved from a distance and at times it is stimulated from past encounters. The fact that someone in the past violated you does not mean that those with whom you currently associate will also violate you. Do not create a situation that causes the present to pay for the past. You owe the past nothing. You paid your dues and you have survived. Your father might have been abusive to your mother, or your mother might have been abusive to your father. This should not give you license to become unjustifiably defensive or unreasonably protective of yourself in your current relationship. Be vigilant, but also be accommodating. An adult who had influence over you as a child might have told you that you would not amount to anything in life, or that you were physically unattractive. Do not allow such inappropriate criticism to hold you captive at this stage of your life. Based on the criticism that they received from others during the most impressionable years of their lives, some incredibly awesome individuals are of the impression that they are unworthy of distinction. They have not been able to reverse that impact of the negative reviews. There is nothing you can do to change the past. Today is a new day and you have the ability to change the narrative from one of self-deprecation to one of self-affirmation. Elevate your self-image!

Put in the required effort to prevent your life from continuing down the path of permitting the past to threaten the staggering growth potential of your present and future. Stop allowing your perceived limitations to stand in the way of your attainable successes. Acquire the necessary support to realign you with your destiny. There is an effective approach that I use in my counseling sessions which I found to be very effective in helping others to reconcile with the past. I would have the counselee sit in a chair and face an empty chair. I would tell my counselee to assume that the person who caused the hurt was sitting in the empty chair. I would then have the counselee confront the notorious offender assertively. A young lady, who suffered years of verbal and physical abuse at the hand of the man she loved, confronted him using the empty chair technique. Initially, she was terrified and reluctant, but as she progressed in her therapy, she became confrontational to the point where she started yelling and screaming at the perpetrator. She had never confronted him in this manner during their relationship. At the end of the session, this counselee expressed a sense of relief and empowerment. We convened several subsequent sessions, and with each session, the counselee became progressively more valiant and assertive. She confirmed that she derived tremendous benefits and insights from the experience. Victims of abuse can become paranoid and repressed to the point of inaction. Confront your entrapments and free yourself!

Life's experiences can make you feel like a hermetically sealed jar with all sorts of repressed energy building up without an opportunity for release. Recovery will only be activated when the lid is removed and the jar is relieved of the pent-up negative energy. You will start experiencing recovery when you remove the lid that entraps the pain imposed upon you from your past experiences. Some of the things that are sunk deep in your psyche are securely buried by layers of heartaches that were never effectively addressed. They might be securely concealed now, but they will eventually find a way to unearth themselves and cause havoc in your mental domain. Your emotions have the tendency to eventually exhume the deeply buried painful experiences and compel you to confront them. If you are not mindful under these circumstances, your emotions could subject you to serious self-destructive responses. Your emotional vulnerabilities have the potential to push you over the cliff, so pay keen attention to the messages that they are sending to you. Get the necessary help and access the appropriate tools you need to break through the barriers that bury your pain. Release the negative emotions precipitated by abuse, hurt, and pain. Be considerate of the messages that your emotions are conveying to you. Accentuate the positive!

Breakthrough

It does not matter how perfect you conceive yourself to be, there will always be someone who disapproves of you. Do not adjust the way you live your life to please others. I will guarantee you that, even if you adjust your life to please others, you will not meet their expectations. You probably tried for many years to live your life to please others and to be accepted into a particular circle. Experience teaches that adjusting your authentic self leaves you unfulfilled and disrespected. Do not spend your valuable time trying to fit into a reality that does not align with your value system. The end does not justify the means. If you are true to yourself, it does not matter what anybody else thinks about you. Square your shoulder, hold your head up high, and move forward. Break through the stifling impositions and show up with your authentic self.

You are an innately good person. Your bad experiences do not define you. Having problems does not mean that you are a problem. Having some bad experiences in your life does not mean that you are a bad person. Do not accept from anyone that you are less than you conceive yourself to be. Sometimes people make unscrupulous assumptions about you and convince themselves and others that their declarations are accurate. Be unfazed by the judgments of others. Never doubt your authenticity for one moment. Believe in who you are. Trust your inner voice. Embrace yourself and stay positive. If you allow your experiences to instruct you, then you adopt a degree of introspection that bolsters your self-concept, strengthens your character and enriches your life. It is crucial to prevent yourself from being pressed out of measure by the cares of life. Disappointments and hurt should never be allowed to prevent you from gaining access to the myriads of positive encounters that await you in the universe. Let the insights you gained from your ordeals drive you towards a brighter day!

Once I was facilitating a session that focused on the impact of our experiences on our current behaviors. One participant disclosed that during the discourse, it occurred to her that she was abused as a child. She revealed that she felt uncomfortable whenever people infringed on her physical space but did not realize the cause until she was engaged in our discourse on the effects of past experience on current behaviors. She did not provide the details, but was able to recall, for the first time, an unsavory experience that she had when she was a child. Sometimes you have to engage in reflective conversations and self-discovery exercises to discover how past encounters have influenced your current behaviors. An understanding of the Johari Window will give insights into the virtues of self-discovery. The Johari Window, a technique developed by psychologists Joseph Luft and Harrington Ingram in 1955, is intended to help people better comprehend their relationship with themselves and others. It suggests that we are viewed from the lenses of four windows. The first window represents the things that we know about ourselves and the things that others know about us. The second window represents the things we know about ourselves, but others do not know about us. The third window represents what others know about us, but we do not know about ourselves. The fourth window represents the things that we do not know about ourselves, and neither do others know about us.

In order to address the blind spots in your life; the things that you do not know about yourself; you must be amenable to receiving feedback from those with whom you are socially and professionally engaged. If you are always getting into conflicts with people, then it could be that you need to make some adjustments in your approach to people. You might want to do a self-reflection and see whether your defiant responses are triggered by past traumatic experiences. I was the victim of bullying in high school, and as a result, I tend to be sensitive to any semblance of intimidation that is directed towards me, or that I witness around me. I am aware that my desire to defend the less fortunate and my defensiveness in the face of inequity, stem from being the victim of bullying in high school. I have learned to give a more objective and empathetic response to those who are construed as having a defensive spirit because I understand the triggers. Your past experiences definitely impact your personality traits. You should embrace feedback and use it for self-evaluation. Make a conscious effort to evolve into a better version of yourself. Upgrade yourself!

Self-Assessment

I once heard the story about a man who was traveling on a very popular highway. As he sped along, he received a call from his wife. She informed him that the news indicated there was a driver speeding in the wrong direction on the highway. She implored him to be very careful. He responded by telling his wife that it is not just one driver but numerous drivers heading in the wrong direction. He further indicated that he was the only driver going in the right direction. It turned out that he was the driver speeding in the wrong direction on the highway. He never stopped to thoroughly evaluate the situation. Have you ever found yourself in a similar predicament? Do you frequently find yourself on the opposing end? Your answers to these questions will be quite telling. It is important to stand up for yourself and to speak truth to power; however, it is also important that you evaluate your position and make sure that you are on the right side of the highway. We all have blind spots; therefore, we should be careful that our judgments are objective. Do you find it difficult to socially integrate? Are you apprehensive in collaborating with others? How do you handle confrontation? Are you afraid to say that you are sorry when you are in the wrong? In order to live your best life, you need to objectively evaluate yourself on a regular basis and make the necessary adjustments in your approach. Your character should be void of conceit. You are not always right. Be objective in your self-judgment!

Be willing to accept both positive and negative feedback from others. Be accepting, and not dismissive, when others attempt to provide you with meaningful feedback. If you become dismissive and cut people off when they are genuinely attempting to help, you will impede your growth and remain stagnated. In order to address your shortfalls that others have identified, be willing to humble yourself and accommodate feedback, even if you are not in agreement with it. Be willing to offer feedback to others, and always be graceful in your delivery. Present it in a manner that you would like for it to be delivered to you. The quality of good feedback has to do with both the fact and the tact with which it is delivered. You can have the fact, but be void of the tact. If there is no tact, then the delivery of the fact may be rejected or disdained by the targeted recipient. So, the fact and the tact are equally important. Be sensitive to people's feelings because you do not know how adversely their past experiences have impacted them. I have mentored many people in my lifetime, and many have demonstrated improvement in their deportment. Some of my mentees have developed into formidable influencers. There are certain individuals with whom I had close association, some for many years, and yet they did not manifest an improvement in their mannerisms. I surmised that these individuals did not benefit from my mentoring primarily because they did not value my feedback. If you want to grow, then you have to be willing to accept your shortcomings and make adjustments in the way you lead your life.

I have had many successes in my life and I have had many disappointments. I have tried to be good to others along the way. I have not always been happy along the journey. I discovered that material things and accomplishments do not fulfill me. Positive psychology suggests that fulfillment and happiness come with being aligned to your values. I do agree with this concept because I have come to realize that my fulfilment is contingent upon how well I am aligned with my core values. I would strongly encourage you to identify your core values and use those values as a roadmap to establish your priorities in life. Be a negotiator and a pursuer of a peaceful and happy existence. In order to live your best life now, you have to be able to effectively navigate the complexities inherent in the establishment of a fulfilling existence. Use the lessons gained from your experiences to empower you to finally live the life you know you deserve. You have been provided with insights into how you can finally live the life you know you deserve. You should make the rest of my days the best of your days. You come first!

Points to Ponder

    a. Face It

       i. Confront every imposition that you faced in life

      ii. Pay attention to the impact of every imposition that occurs in your life

     iii. Acknowledge the impact of every imposition in your life

    b. Feel It

       i. Endure the impact of every imposition that occurs in your life

      ii. Scrutinize the impact of every imposition that occurs in your life

     iii. Make meaning of every imposition that occurs in your life

    c. Accept It

       i. Develop a tolerance for the impact of every imposition that occurs in your life

      ii. Consider the value of every imposition that occurs in your life

     iii. Be thankful for the experiences gleaned from the imposition in your life

d. Own It

    i.   Consider every imposition a contributor to your growth and development

    ii.   Consider every imposition a contributor to your strength and fortitude

    iii.   Consider every imposition a compliment to your character

e. Manipulate It

    i.   Document what you have learned for your reference

    ii.   Leverage what you have learned for your betterment

    iii.   Establish what you have learned for the benefit of others

Opening of your heart lends itself to hopefulness and myriads of possibilities, but it also carries along with it the risk of attracting hurtful and harmful possibilities. Closing your heart to hopefulness and possibilities can stifle the prospects of a greater tomorrow. Choose wisely.

Reflections

_____

_____

_____

_____

_____

_____

_____

_____

_____

_____

_____

_____

_____

_____

_____

_____

_____

PONDERINGS

People's true character will be manifested in the way they treat you once their intended needs have been met.

The act of ungratefulness is among the lowest forms of human indecency.

Trust your gut feeling. It is the most accurate navigator of human complexities.

When your abnormality becomes your normalcy, then the details of your destiny will become distorted.

The bad thing that happens to you is not a judgment on your character; it is a propeller designed to push you towards becoming a better version of yourself.

Living your truth does not warrant a public display of your resolve.

Made in the USA
Middletown, DE
10 March 2022

62328825R00129